STOKING
THE FIRE OF
DEMOCRACY

Praise for **Stoking the Fire of Democracy**

Reading *Stoking the Fire of Democracy* is like talking to the part of yourself that tells you to risk more, dream bigger, push harder. It's a primer for a generation of young organizers and activists who lifted the most unlikely presidential candidate in U.S. history to victory and finds itself asking, "What's the next earth-shattering thing we can do?"

Eboo Patel, Founder and Executive Director,
Interfaith Youth Core

Stephen Smith, in word and deed, has shown himself a young leader worth following. A new generation is coming of age, beginning to flex their democratic muscles and find a voice in the public square. *Stoking the Fire of Democracy* tells that story and paints a vision for what is still coming. Whether you are a young person looking to step into the world of grassroots organizing or a seasoned veteran looking for hope, refreshment and new insight, read this book cover to cover and make sure it is a well-worn volume in your library.

Jim Wallis, author, The Great Awakening,
Editor-in-Chief, Sojourners Magazine

We young people often confuse mistakes as failures when, in fact, they are life's best lessons. *Stoking the Fire of Democracy* is a collage of candid stories that demonstrates mistakes, risks and successes from which we should all learn if we truly believe in grassroots movements. It provides us with the tools to go beyond activism and the challenge to be real agents of social change. Stephen Smith's work reminds me of why I love organizing.

Jamiko Rose, Lead Organizer,
Organization of the North East (ONE)

Activism and organizing can feel like a giant hamster wheel—lots of effort, no movement. Stephen Smith's brilliant little book will teach you to rig helicopter blades to your hamster wheel and achieve lift-off. Barack Obama called community organizing "the best education I ever got." Stephen Smith, one of the next generation's most brilliant organizers, followed Obama's footsteps to Chicago and emerged with a compulsively readable little book that will change your life. *Stoking the Fire of Democracy* will light a fire under the ass of our generation.

Ben Wikler, Co-Director, Avaaz.org

In an age of cynicism, fear and doubt, Stephen Smith's work calls us back to faith. It is a clarion call to all classes and generations to believe again that social change is possible. Faith, humility, and hard work, coupled with a little compassion, represent a potent combination. I have been inspired to roll up my sleeves one more time.

Theodore Williams, Professor of Political Science,
Kennedy-King College

Stoking the Fire of Democracy is a must-read for all community organizers, social-change agents, and those who simply wonder about their own ability to make a difference. This book will keep the fire in your belly burning. Smith lays out an honest and methodical approach to organizing—one that is invaluable to sustaining any kind of change. The spark of brilliance in this book comes from Smith's affirmation that failure is an option, and that the courage to fail is the truest indicator of dedication and success in this field. This book should remain a staple in the world of community organizing.

Paul Rieckhoff, Executive Director,
Iraq and Afghanistan Veterans of America

STOKING
THE FIRE OF
DEMOCRACY

Our generation's
introduction to
grassroots organizing

Stephen Noble Smith

acta
PUBLICATIONS

STOKING THE FIRE OF DEMOCRACY
Our Generation's Introduction to Grassroots Organizing
by Stephen Noble Smith

Edited by Gregory F. Augustine Pierce
Cover by Tom A. Wright
Text design and typesetting by Patricia A. Lynch

Published by ACTA Publications, 5559 W. Howard Street,
Skokie, IL 60077-2621, (800) 397-2282, www.actapublications.com

Library of Congress Catalog number: 2009933087
ISBN: 978-0-87946-414-1
Printed in Canada by Graphics TwoFortyFour, Inc.
Year 20 19 18 17 16 15 14 13 12 11 10 09
Printing 15 14 13 12 11 10 9 8 7 6 5 4 3 2 First

♻ Text printed on 100% post-consumer recycled paper

CONTENTS

To Ed Chambers

Executive Director of the Industrial Areas Foundation,
mentor and trainer to many could-be radicals, including me,
and grassroots organizer for over fifty-five years.

INTRODUCTION
WHAT WILL WE FIGHT FOR?

In democratic countries,
knowledge of how to combine
is the mother of all other forms of knowledge;
on its progress depends that of all the others.

Alexis de Tocqueville,
Democracy in America

My first day as an organizer my boss told me, "I don't fire people for making mistakes. I fire people for not making mistakes."

This book is about what de Tocqueville called "combining," what we today call "organizing." It is written for young people like me who are trying to figure out what we are willing to fight for and how to be effective while maintaining our integrity.

When Barack Obama was elected president of the United States in 2008 at the age of 47, he became the first leader of our country who started his political career as a community organizer. While Obama did not stick with grassroots organizing of the kind I am going to describe in this book (opting instead for the practice of law and then electoral politics), he used many of his organizing skills and talents to run his campaign and then assemble his government. Obama didn't learn this stuff at Harvard. (I know; I went there.) He learned it on the street.

Most of the real knowledge any of us has comes from trying and failing. From loads of mistakes. It comes from testing our boundaries, from doing things that make us uncomfortable. At its best, this book is a primer on taking risks and learning from mistakes.

For four years after college, I was an organizer with the Industrial Areas Foundation (IAF). The IAF is a network of grassroots citizen organizations across the U.S. (with sister organizations in Canada, Germany, and the U.K.). In cities like Los Angeles, San Antonio, Milwaukee, Winston-Salem, Spokane and Phoenix, people from religious congregations and other "third sector" institutions (health centers, universities, etc.) are combining to fight for common concerns and the common good. IAF organizations built 4000 affordable homes in New York, won a living wage in Baltimore, and brought universal health care to Massachusetts.

The IAF hired me to try and build one of these organizations in Chicago. With a catch. The organization would be created and led by young adults (ages 15-35), a first for the IAF. The young adult leaders named the organization Public Action for Change Today (PACT) to represent their commitment to building power together across the race, class and faith differences that normally divided them. PACT wrote legislation that won health care for thousands of young adults, brokered relationships between youth and police, and helped win back state financial aid cuts for working-class kids. After, and largely thanks to, a lot of failures along the way, the organization was successful and I learned enough to believe I could write this book.

Conventional wisdom reasons we should wait "our turn" to run things. Maybe so. But maybe not.

It is presumptuous of me to do so. I don't have enough knowledge or experience to write *the* book on organizing. But I might have enough to write *our* book on organizing. There's something to be said for writing about a journey which hasn't yet ended. And maybe you're reading this because it was written by someone like you who hasn't got everything figured out. Someone like you who's skeptical of the conventional wisdom that says we should hedge our bets, that we should do the safe thing, the thing that makes money—instead of doing the thing we love or fighting the things that make us angry. Conventional wisdom reasons we should wait "our turn" to run things. Maybe so. But maybe not.

I left PACT after four years to study at the London School of Economics and to write this book while it was still fresh in my mind and when it could be useful to my fellow "could-be radicals," as I will refer to us here. It doesn't really matter to me if you agree with me. (Among other things, organizing taught me that agreement is overrated.) As I keep making mistakes, I am likely to change my own mind about the ideas in this book. But I offer them here as a challenge to you and as a starting point for action.

I am an organizer because first I was a loser. In high school in Plano, Texas, I lost four consecutive student government elections. With nothing left to unsuccessfully run for, two buddies and I got together and formed a service group at our school. We called it GSI (Getting Students Involved), and it attracted 800 students and generated thousands of dollars and volunteer hours. There was a Charity Garage Sale and a Charity Basketball Tournament, frequent visits to a local shelter, and a campus beautification day. We butted heads with the school administration because we let anybody join and rarely went through "the proper channels." My first organizing lesson: go do what you think is right. Regardless.

I went from Plano to Cambridge (Massachusetts, that is) to earn my undergraduate degree at Harvard. There I found other young people like me who wanted to make the world a better place in ways more thrilling than Charity Garage Sales. We were a loose cadre of students who believed we could learn more outside of a classroom than inside it. We built a group called "Har'd CORPS" to put on service days and fundraisers and to challenge students to make longer-term commitments to volunteerism. We started BASIC, a link for Boston campuses to initiate joint service projects. We fought for a living wage for campus service workers, better rape prevention programs at the university, global AIDS funding, and an end to Harvard's contribution to sweatshop labor overseas. We won about half the time, which means we lost the other half.

The living wage campaign at Harvard is a good snapshot of the highs and lows I faced as a student activist. We held dozens of rallies, teach-ins, and worker appreciation days, and eventually we took over the administration building for twenty-one days. We won a base wage of $11.35/hour plus benefits for all campus workers, but the University never agreed to the principle of a living wage—leaving them wiggle room to cut wages down the road. We were long on energy but often short on smarts. We talked about the importance of human dignity but didn't always take care of one another, letting ourselves burn out. We had some good leaders but paid little more than lip service to the development and training of a next generation of activists. We had the opportunity to build a lasting relationship between campus workers and students. But in this most important endeavor, we ran out of steam and know-how.

Our shortcomings were glaring: weak strategy, not much leadership development, no long-term vision. In our world, you had to be an "activist" to do activism. Too often we fostered a culture that made it difficult for students (or workers) who were not as ideological or committed as we thought we were to join us. We took pride in not being in the mainstream. To our detriment, we failed to learn from those who swam there every day.

So-called "service work" frustrated me just as much. I spent my summers as the children's program coordinator for Family Gateway, a transitional shelter in Dallas. There I tried to emulate the deep passion and soulfulness of my mentor, an underappreciated and remarkable woman named Dot Brown. Despite all I learned from her, it still made me angry how little we were able to change the circumstances that led to homelessness.

In both student activism and direct service, one thing was constant: Power flowed from the top down. Privileged students or white service board members were running programs or campaigns for poor folks. I remember thinking: How can we really change the world if we are not all equals in the fight?

After graduation from Harvard, I received a grant and took my jumble of frustration to Botswana, a small, landlocked, African country just north of South Africa. My goal was to learn how a different culture was fighting the highest rate of AIDS infection in the world. The U.N. claimed that 20-30 percent of Botswana's adults were infected with the virus, but this was a rough estimate. Most people in Botswana who were infected didn't know it. And they weren't trying to find out because: 1) there is such a stigma attached to the disease, 2) there were not enough drugs available to help anyway, 3) they did not trust the services provided by their government, 4) they did not know the doctors, and 5) the programs are "parachuted in" from overseas. I went to Botswana to learn how another culture approached social change; instead, I saw another version of the problems I had experienced in the States.

The results of the anti-AIDS efforts in Botswana scared me. Smart, passionate people with resources—experts from across the globe—were trying very hard to stop the spread of the virus and treat those already infected. As with our cadre at Harvard, they made strides, but they fought a losing battle. The infection rate was not going down; the drug programs were not catching on. Botswana taught me that social change is not so much about figuring out the right solutions as it is about who wages the fight. As much as they tried, talented foreigners could not solve the AIDS problem in Botswana. In many ways, our presence stunted the emergence of local leadership, which was the worst possible outcome I could imagine.

The strange thing is that, looking back, Botswana taught me more about what was right with the world than what was wrong.

The most lasting lesson from my time in Botswana was that the appearance of doing good work is not the same thing as making the world a better place.

Watching a village spend three days grieving the death of one of its members taught me about solidarity. Living in a culture that values friendship and leisure a little more (and work a little less) taught me about the importance of joy. Working with folks who saw service organizations more like uncles than government programs taught me about family and the limits of state-provided social and health services. Yet while I was there none of the expatriates, including me, ever really spoke about what we could learn from Botswana—only what was wrong with the country and its people.

During the four months I spent in Botswana, I wrote grants for education and prevention organizations. I served as the event manager for the government's World AIDS Day commemoration, which sought to educate people about services they could seek. I spent an afternoon each week at a daycare for the children of young mothers. I teamed up with activists to win youth representation in national AIDS advocacy organizations. But I was in over my head. The most lasting lesson from my time there was that the appearance of doing good work is not the same thing as making the world a better place.

I realized there was much more I needed to learn. I wanted to learn how to agitate and organize people to fight for their own interests, to build power for themselves rather than just accept projects started and owned by others. And I felt I needed to do something in my own country before I could tell anyone else what to do in theirs.

So back in the United States, I linked up with the Foundation for Civic Leadership and spent six months creating a Summer Institute for twenty-five student activists from around the country. I used the opportunity to attempt to understand and then teach the lessons I had learned from my own confused experiences. But I was still going a hundred miles an hour. There were a few victories, and some good training took place, but I had more questions than answers. The program was temporary, national, intellectual, and for privileged college kids. This was not the long haul, cross-class, multi-cultural transformation I sought.

Around that same time, I realized that not one of the things I had helped start—GSI in high school, BASIC and the Living Wage Campaign in college, a little activist coalition in Botswana—was still thriving. This made me sick to my stomach.

While preparing for the Summer Institute, a friend invited me to a ten-day training session organized by the Industrial Areas Foundation (IAF). I had been to many conferences before, and I did not expect much.

At the IAF training, however, I met a group of people much like myself. They weren't all young adults; many had started working for justice before I was born. More than anything, what struck me was this: I had never seen so many people from different race and class backgrounds actually treating one another as equals. These were parents and teachers and pastors and laypeople who were sticking up for their families and communities. They preached that relationships (not principles or ideas) come before action; and they practiced what they preached. Hours each day during the training were set aside for face-to-face, one-to-one meetings between the participants. No one was doing anything for anybody else. We were all in this together—listening to one another's stories.

I learned that, at least for the IAF, "combining" happens one conversation at a time. But was it only conversation?

It wasn't. During another part of the training, we all went to a nearby convention hall. A local IAF organization had approached their state's governor to address particular problems. The governor agreed to most of the organization's (notably specific) requests—on issues ranging from education to immigrant labor to health centers. The meeting was obviously planned from gavel to gavel, but it wasn't paid organizers or staff people who were running the "action," as they called it. It was volunteer leaders from the organization's member institutions. The audience, 1200 strong on a Sunday afternoon, represented every neighborhood and religious tradition in the area. The speakers addressed issues that affected them personally, in prepared and practical public statements. What blew my mind was the discipline. Everyone kept to the agenda and the timetable, including the governor. This was not the kind of four-hour marathon meeting I was used to running or attending. The event succeeded because it was owned and led by hundreds of local people who were there with their families. It occurred to me that that's what happens when relationships come before action.

My notes from the training are filled with bold-print epiphanies: PEOPLE BEFORE IDEAS...BE CURIOUS...TAKE RISKS. Towards the end of the ten-day training, Ed Chambers (the IAF national director) spoke about the IAF's history. At the end of his remarks, he said he was looking for someone who could build an experimental organization based in Chicago focusing on young adults. That turned out to be PACT, and I turned out to be its initial organizer.

What drew me to Chambers at first was that he seemed wholly allergic to bullshit. At his request, I had written an evaluation of the ten-day training and sent it to him. When I walked into his Chicago office two months later to interview for the job, I had nearly forgotten about my initial remarks. Chambers had not. There was no "hello," no "thanks for making the trip out from Boston," no "how were your holidays?" He took out my evaluation, dumped it in front of me, pointed to the first thing I had written, and said, "You got this all wrong."

Chambers taught me that real radicals exist in between the world-as-it-is and the world-as-it-could-be.

I worked with Chambers for about four years. He was the first person who really cared enough about me to agitate and mentor me. I owe him a lot, which is why this book is dedicated to him.

Chambers taught me that real radicals exist *in between* the world-as-it-is and the world-as-it-could-be. In a group of ideologues and optimists, the radical is a pragmatist. In a group of skeptics and pessimists, the radical is the visionary. Or as Saul Alinsky wrote in 1946, a radical "believes intensely in the possibilities of man and hopes fervently for the future" while "[recognizing] that constant dissension and conflict is and has been the fire under the boiler of democracy." A *radical* is a true *agent of change*. I'll use the term *could-be radicals* for those of us who want to organize at a grassroots level but are still learning our way.

This book is for us could-be radicals—young adults, like me, who seek the world-as-it-could-be and who are willing to make some mistakes in the world-as-it-is in order to get there.

Stephen Noble Smith
Chicago, Illinois

CHAPTER ONE
FINDING OUR "WHY"

How do I know about the world?
By what is within me.

Tao Teh Ching

We can learn a lot from four-year-olds. Around age four, most kids first encounter the notion of cause and effect. They realize things don't just happen; they happen for a reason.

Kids are awed by this. Rightly so. You hear it in their one-word mantra: "Why? Why? Why? Why?"

The question "Why?" serves us could-be radicals too. We ask it of potential allies and targets often. But we start here by asking it of ourselves.

Why? Why get involved in social change at all? Why care about making the world a better place? Why fight? And for what?

Even at its best, the work of social change is tough. Not only will we lose, but we will lose often—and in public. We need strength to withstand the inevitable setbacks and pitfalls of organizing. Knowing why we do what we do helps us make both strategic (long range) and tactical (short range) decisions. It guides us toward what really matters and away from what doesn't. Knowing our "why" helps us understand that it's not just *what* we do but *how* we do it that matters. Most importantly, knowing why we do things allows us to communicate who we are to others.

Defeat and frustration will find us—whether we are slogging through a campaign for a new neighborhood playground or lobbying for recycling services or opposing a popular war. Knowing why we do what we do keeps us going when we would rather be doing almost anything else.

Thich Nhat Hanh, the Buddhist thinker and activist, once wrote: "the raft is not the shore." The journey is not the destination. The struggle is not the outcome. Activists of every stripe tend to talk a lot about shores, destinations and outcomes, but our "why" is our raft, the thing that keeps us afloat long enough so that we might just reach our goals.

Scimone Edwards was a nineteen-year-old, homeless, single mother when she faced the prospect of speaking in public for the first time. She was to tell her story of homelessness to an audience at a local community college that included a state legislator, college students, other homeless youth, and ex-offenders. At the end of her speech, she would ask the legislator to sponsor legislation creating transitional jobs for homeless young adults.

But at this moment, just before the meeting, Ms. Edwards was scared. Another leader, Andre McDearmon, an ex-offender who was chairing the meeting, let her know that we would support her however it went. And then he asked her, "Why did you want to do this in the first place?"

For Edwards, knowing her "why" had nothing to do with harrowing statistics or arguments about the cycles of poverty. Her "why" was her son and her wish that he have opportunities that were unavailable to her. She carried her "why" with her every day—to job interviews, to daycare centers, to meetings with caseworkers. She didn't know it in her head; she knew it in her gut.

Ms. Edwards's son was not her only "why." Her mother had kicked her out of the house; she wanted to prove her mother wrong. Her social worker had stayed after work to help her with her speech; she wanted to prove her social worker right. She also knew that she needed and wanted a job as soon as possible. So in addition to asking for new legislation, she decided to ask the state legislator—and everyone else in attendance at the meeting—to help her find a job.

Our "whys" are usually complicated and deeply personal. But when we know what really matters to us, what drives us, what our passions are, we make better decisions. Knowing our "why" helps us understand and navigate our own self-interest.

Rene Delgado was a twenty-year-old student when he joined Public Action for Change Today (PACT), a new group of young adult could-be radicals in Chicago. The son of immigrants, he thought a lot about how he could honor his parents, their culture, and the sacrifices they had made. Underneath his waist-length hair and Che t-shirt, Mr. Delgado was at his core a devoted son. He also suffered from a chronic illness.

Delgado's sense of urgency was almost palpable. Upon hearing of PACT's nascent campaigns (on immigration, health care, financial aid), Delgado joined them all.

That was his problem: He'd do anything. For a while, you could not attend a PACT meeting without seeing Mr. Delgado— and it literally wore him out. During a one-on-one conversation, I challenged him to do only the one thing he was most passionate about and let other folks take responsibility for the rest. He surprised me with his decision to focus on reinstating financial aid for college students in Illinois. Even though this young man had his own schooling paid for by scholarships and grants, his best friend was trying to raise kids, work, and go to school, and Delgado knew she might have to drop out of classes if we could not win back her financial aid.

Knowing our "why" informs how we relate to people within and outside our own communities. But it's not enough to know it. We have to share it too. This potent little act of vulnerability —telling our dreams and deficiencies to people we don't know well, and asking them to do the same—fuels organizing. These moments of mutual vulnerability/accountability form the basis of strong relationships and often lead to action.

Let's flesh this out a little more. If you share with me your "why"—your struggle, the people and things that matter to you, what wakes you up in the morning—then I can imagine myself in your position. Whether we live on the same side of the tracks or not, we can relate.

When we trust each other not to laugh at our aspirations but to hold one another accountable for them, we take a risk. But it sure beats the alternative: building our relationships—as we normally do—on the flimsier stuff of convenience and commonality.

Connie Garrett is a black sociology professor in her thirties. She struck me initially as antagonistic, indefatigable, hopeful, emotional, and very much an ideologue. She hurried everywhere. She was a fan of big dreams and sweeping generalizations.

My read on Ms. Garrett was simple (and simplistic). I felt she had too much head and not enough heart. Like many could-be radicals, she was committed to ideas and ideals, but that made it hard for her to operate in the world as it is. I worried how she would react when the inevitable obstacles arose and she would be forced to compromise. I figured she would fold under that pressure.

Ms. Garrett proved me wrong. Through hard work, she won a spot in our summer-long organizing class for top emerging leaders. At first, she battled with others in the class and frequently painted herself as a naysayer. In one activity, participants were asked to draw a stick figure of themselves and write in rank order the things that are most important to them (for example: my son, my struggle for citizenship, having enough money to support myself, my faith in God, my mother who is sick). Garrett was the only student in the class not to list a single other person on her stick figure; it was all ideas ("I want a justice-oriented community," etc.).

One of the last class sessions focused on the importance of storytelling in achieving social change. A veteran leader gave some examples, and the students were asked to relate one personal story that helped answer the "why" question: "Why are you taking this class? Why do you want to change your community?" They had twenty minutes to write a story that would help answer "why?".

Ms. Garrett's story started with her mother. They were close, she said, and she lived to impress her mom. They came from poverty, and she wanted to get into the University of Chicago to prove herself. Her mother had been so proud when she was admitted, but Ms. Garrett had to turn down the offer because of the cost. She said she had taken the organizing class to continue to prove herself to her mother. She talked about going to college in Texas and fighting the administration for better treatment of minority students, and how she and her fellow students had failed. She said she had taken the class so she would not fail the next time. She talked about living in New Orleans and being displaced by the storm, about feeling helpless and sidetracked when she came back to Chicago. These truths just poured out of her, in story form. She spoke uninterrupted for nearly twenty minutes, eliciting tears and laughter from her classmates (and from me).

That moment did not completely change my judgment of Ms. Garrett. But it forced me to put myself in her position. It allowed me to see some of the experiences that had made her who she is. It encouraged me to see how she could continue to develop, rather than how she was likely to fail.

Finally, it hit me: Until then, Garrett and I had never really done the essential relational work with each other—learning about where we came from and what matters to us. I had failed in the most important step in organizing: I had failed to share *my* "why" and be curious about *hers*. Perhaps we both deserved blame, but I was supposed to be the professional organizer and I had forgotten to do my relational work. She may not have opened up, but neither had I.

Telling someone what really matters to us is one of the most radical things we can do in public life. It may also be the most important. Even if you believe this to be true (as I did), and even if your "why" is something you have thought a lot about (as Ms. Garrett had), our tendency is to skip over these conversations in favor of something safer, to spend more time writing mass e-mails and less time sitting across from someone face-to-face. This book is about what happens when two people of different backgrounds take the chance to let each other in.

Telling someone what really matters to us is one of the most radical things we can do in public life.

Learning what matters to us, and to each other, means taking risks over and over again. When we think we have a handle on one of the stories or memories or relationships that really motivates us, we must take it out for a spin. We must tell others what matters to us. We need to hear how it sounds to us and to them. Then we have to ask others what matters to them and listen to what they say. Their answers often hold truths for us too. Like most worthwhile things, finding our "why" takes time and reflection, action and evaluation. And when we feel as though we have a hold on it, it will change.

The word *interest* owes its origin to the Latin *inter esse*, meaning "to be between or among others." The Romans understood one of public life's many paradoxes: Your self-interest (another way of saying your "why")—though totally personal—is only fully realized in relationship to others.

- Scimone Edwards not only needed her son to help her find the courage to speak out in public; she also needed Andre McDearmon's encouragement.
- Rene Delgado's "why" was to fight alongside his best friend.
- Connie Garrett was tired of going it alone; her "why" was finding allies and mentors to support her.

And my "why" was to get into relationship and action with real people like them, who were willing to let a young, white, middle-class, Harvard-educated idealist be part of their lives.

What's your "why"?

CHAPTER TWO
HOW NOT TO BE
A LONELY ORGANIZER

*Always remember
that you are absolutely unique.
Just like everyone else.*

Margaret Mead

This chapter could be summed up, 1 + 1 > 2.

In the Hebrew Scriptures, the prophet Elijah was on the run from Queen Jezebel, who had sworn an oath to kill him. He ran through the desert for forty days before he came to Mount Horeb. There an angel told him that God would soon pass by. When God arrived, he asked Elijah "What are you doing here?" Elijah replied that he was alone and afraid. He had done all he could to fight the priests of Baal, but no one would listen to him. God told him to get off his duff and go find someone else to work with him. And then God gave him directions on where to find the person who turned out to be his partner and ultimate replacement, the prophet Elisha.

Elijah knew his "why" (first, to survive; and second, to keep fighting the priests of Baal to preserve his own religion). He just needed to find somebody else to help him out.

My regrets from my organizing to date come in one of two forms: untaken risks and selfish acts. Maybe this book will encourage you (and me) to stop doing these things so much. Maybe we will take more risks (Chapter 4), and maybe we will learn how to think not only of ourselves.

A 19-year-old student at North Park University in Chicago heard about PACT's campaign to win bus passes for homeless youth. She wanted to help.

At the time, I was obsessed with scheduling as many meetings as possible between young people and their city council representatives (in Chicago they're called "aldermen"), because this was the strategy we had adopted. So I gave this student the green light to schedule a meeting with her alderman, even though I knew almost nothing about her (except that she was in favor of bus passes for homeless youth) and absolutely nothing about her alderman. I figured I would go with her, so how bad could it be?

The meeting was a disaster. The alderman berated her for not yet being registered to vote (which I did not know). He reserved even harsher judgment for me for not having registered her to vote before I dragged her in to meet with him (especially because our own literature referred to us as a "young-voter organization"). While it's true that the alderman was no Mr. Congeniality, I could have (and should have) been better prepared. I wasn't. I could see only my personal goal or task. There was nothing else, no one else.

And because I failed to think about this student and prepare her well for the meeting, neither of us got what we wanted. The organization did not achieve its goal of getting bus passes for homeless youth. Worst of all, though unsurprising, the young woman never showed up for another meeting of our group. She had trusted me with her first foray into public life, and it was horrible. I can only hope she found some other outlet for her desire to do good. We both paid the price for my selfishness.

This kind of selfishness is tempting. Here's how it works: I get passionate about something (such as youth homelessness in our cities); I know what I want to see happen; I think I know how to get there; so I recruit people to help me carry out my vision. I see how people might be able to fit into a campaign, and I convince myself that because they *can* fit, they must also *want* to fit. If my agenda is altruistic, then they must want it as well.

This pattern of imposing our will on others wears many masks: manipulation, charisma, personality cults. When we want people to do something that they do not really want to do for themselves, they might follow us for a little while. But pretty soon they will feel used, get bored, and quit. Or, even worse from an organizing standpoint, they will come to need us to do things they could well do for themselves.

Selfishness has an evil twin—equally as tempting and equally problematic. It's sometimes called "service," but here we use the word selflessness. If selfishness is all about me; selflessness is all about you. Either way, someone gets subtracted from the equation. Selflessness goes something like this: "It's not about me; it's about them—the poor, the at-risk, the unfortunate. I have it so lucky, I just want to do what I can to help people less fortunate than me." As with selfishness, good things can (and often do) come from selflessness. Hospitals get built and campaigns get won and businesses get formed by egomaniacs and saints alike.

If selfishness is all about me; selflessness is all about you. Either way, someone gets subtracted from the equation.

But selflessness has its problems, and those problems mirror the problems of selfishness. Rather than subjugating someone else's humanity (selfishness), we subjugate our own humanity when we do for others exclusively (selflessness). The lesson we teach when we are selfless is that things come for free. Worse yet, we rob someone of the opportunity to help *us*; we rob someone of the opportunity to know us as an equal.

It is this last condition of selflessness that contains a counterintuitive air of superiority. Selflessness often comes with the unspoken subtext: "I know what you want or need better than you do."

My experience as an AIDS worker in Botswana taught me how hard it is to get past the twin temptations of selfishness and selflessness. How could one possibly build an "equal" partnership between well-funded and well-educated foreigners on the one hand and local teachers, doctors, and religious leaders on the other? How could I overcome my lack of knowledge and experience, do some good, and also allow myself to learn from local folks? My failures were legion. I managed to help win an extra grant for one local organization that ended up using it to hire more foreigners and drift further away from the communities in which they were based. I helped assemble a youth AIDS action team that created some hope and goodwill that proved hollow after I left. I met good-hearted Americans with grandiose titles like "Behavior Change Specialist." They seemed set-up to fail.

Misguided selflessness may be the rule in international aid, but there are exceptions. We have heroes in our generation—like the team at Avaaz.org who are re-writing the rules of international engagement by creating alliances of action among people across the world with a common interest in holding governments accountable. They succeed more than they fail by working with local leaders to call—not for charity—but rather for solidarity based on shared interests and values, launching initiatives in which citizens of rich and poor countries alike both give and receive.

Notably, the project I enjoyed most in Botswana was also the simplest: I volunteered once each week at an orphanage. It was an easy trade: I gave the staff a respite; in return, I got to re-energize by playing with two year olds.

Selflessness and selfishness both undermine the likelihood of creating mutual respect and dignity. If my relationship with you is predicated on the notion that I'm privileged and you are not (or vice versa), how can we together build an organization, or a movement, based on equality?

There is a saying: "Give a man a fish, he eats for a day. Teach a man to fish, he eats for a lifetime." There is truth here, but it misses the main point. In both cases (giving and teaching), one person (the giver/teacher) is supposedly greater than the other (the fledgling fisherman).

Some organizers modify the quote: "Give man a fish, he eats for a day. Teach a man to fish, and he eats until the local factory pollutes his lake. Teach a man to organize, and he eats for a lifetime." This alteration falls short for the same reason. Across these scenarios, the fisherman and the giver/teacher/organizer are never equals. Let's dig deeper.

Selflessness and selfishness both undermine the likelihood of creating mutual respect and dignity.

Mutual self-interest is our best weapon against selfishness and selflessness. And it's hard as hell. It requires us to be 1) curious about, and respectful of, the interests of those we meet; 2) honest about our own interests; and 3) imaginative about how we might achieve mutual interests together. Mutual self-interest is the bedrock of organizing.

Mutual self-interest makes intuitive sense. Your first grade math teacher taught you that 1 + 1 equals 2. But in the world of social change, 1 + 1 can be more than 2. If two people combine their individual interests and make themselves vulnerable to each other, their power can increase by more than the sum of their individual parts. Mutual self-interest is not only an ideal worth striving for in principle, it is also the most practical way to achieve power, and power is the purpose of organizing. Mutual self-interest is, in the final analysis, the only way to achieve the common good.

In the Chicago community organization PACT, an orthodox Jew, a Muslim and an evangelical Christian joined together, out of mutual self-interest, to run a voter registration drive.

Max Kuecker, the Christian, linked up with Ahmed Zedan, the Muslim, and Matt Wetstein, the Jew, because they each wanted to get the attention of the next governor of Illinois. More people = more voters = more likelihood of getting a politician's attention. Each man wanted to increase the political involvement of his own group, and each wanted to have the ear of the next governor on issues of importance to him—whether homelessness (Max), substance abuse and ex-offender issues (Ahmed), or health care (Matt). By uniting forces and committing to hold one another accountable, they were all able to better achieve their aims. The campaign worked because each of them (and other key leaders) fostered relationships of mutual self-interest. All wanted to see increased voter registration or political participation in their own churches/mosques/synagogues.

In contrast, the first time PACT tried a voter registration campaign, it failed. Put simply, we had not taken the time to help people cultivate their own self-interests and find a connection to the self-interests of others. We were all operating under either selfishness (we wanted people to buy into our agenda for what we perceived to be the common good) or selflessness (we would do whatever we perceived others wanted to do). Our "why" did not go beyond "it seems like a good idea." Absent was the gut-level pride (based on identity) that fueled the second campaign built on mutual self-interest. When that first campaign inevitably faltered, the leaders themselves lacked the energy and relationships with one another to pull it back together.

So, why did Wetstein, Kuecker and Zedan succeed? Why doesn't their kind of collaboration happen more often? If mutual self-interest makes intuitive sense, leads to success, and builds a foundation for respect and equality down the road, why is it not the norm? Because organizing this way requires us to give up things we don't want to part with: our time, our vulnerability, our privacy, our control, and some of our beliefs.

Mutual self-interest takes time, lots of it. It takes time for me to understand your interests. It takes time for me to open myself up to you and for you to listen. It takes time for the two of us to imagine how our interests might coincide. And mostly, it takes time to build the kind of organization based on trust that is required to move forward on behalf of our shared interests.

At some point, most of us could-be radicals ask this question: "Why doesn't everybody just work together?" For a few months or a few years, we get on our soapbox. We tell all who will listen that if only everybody who cared about this issue or that issue would work together, we could change the world. We accept humbly the mantle of "connector"—the one who is trying to connect everybody in this divided world. We advocate things like "networking events" and "dialogues" and "conferences." In college, I did all of these things. All I had to show for it was the so-called Progressive Alliance—which lasted four whole meetings —and a couple other student groups that started with great ideas but ended by the time I graduated.

Turns out there's a reason why we don't all just work together: It's really hard. Indeed, we could-be radicals have it harder than could-be activists, who thrive on the gratification of doing some-thing—anything—to show their anger, or could-be ideologues, who build worlds out of ideas and arguments. Frustrated with the ideologues' and activists' absolutes, we radicals choose far messier territory "in-between": in-between the world-as-it-is and the world-as-it-could-be; in-between pragmatism and pas-sion; and, most importantly, in-between you and me. We try our best to choose the more compli-cated stuff of relationships upon which to build our power.

Turns out there's a reason why we don't all just work together: It's really hard.

Wetstein, Kuecker and Zedan only agreed to collaborate in such a big way because they had developed a relationship over time. They attended meetings together on smaller campaigns and witnessed how each reliably lived up to the commitments he made. They had participated in a weekend retreat where they had time to brainstorm together. And they had tested the idea of a massive Voter Power Campaign for young adults on other leaders in PACT and in their own religious institutions. After the three of them agreed to move forward with the campaign, Kuecker and Zedan volunteered to hash out the final strategy. At their first meeting, they spent two hours talking about their backgrounds and their own "whys." They intuitively understood that they needed to know each other better before they set pen to paper.

Collective action requires the patience to build up trust over time, and time is the thing most of us do not think we have.

Collective action also requires aligning ourselves with people who are different from us in fundamental ways. One of the advantages of selfishness and selflessness is that both are relatively safe. Selfishness involves a single-mindedness of purpose that is invigorating and protective. "I have to achieve this goal, and I will not let you or anyone else stand in my way." If this is truly my attitude, then I do not have to take seriously the criticisms or concerns of others.

Inversely, the selfless person is also shielded from criticism by putting the burden on the people he or she is trying to help. "I am here to help you; that's my only job." If you ask me why I am helping you or if you try to find out what I am struggling with in my life, I can automatically deflect you...because it's not about me. This denial of self has many serious side effects, not the least of which is burnout. We could-be radicals need all the energy we can conjure in this work, and it's no use denying ourselves the reservoir of our own joys, dreams and calamities.

Selfishness and selflessness offer avenues of escape. Because we do not have to take seriously either someone else's point of view or our own interests, we can hide from criticism and vulnerability. It is one thing to know why and how we want to change the world. It is something different to share those passions with others, making ourselves vulnerable to their judgment or criticism. It can also be risky asking others to open themselves up to our judgment.

Finally, selfishness and selflessness allow us to keep control. But collective power requires that we give up control from time to time. We put our fates partly in the hands of others and accept their fates as our own. Mutual self-interest means people work to achieve their ends together. Wetstein, Kuecker and Zedan were able to learn from one another and hold one another accountable. As a result, each achieved his aim. They all worked together, and each got what he wanted. $1 + 1 + 1 = 3$.

But earlier we said the sum could be greater than the parts. Here's how: Because each man also made himself vulnerable—that is, open to accountability and criticism from the others—he also achieved more than he originally intended. Wetstein gained an appreciation for a Muslim perspective in the Israel-Palestine conflict from Zedan. Zedan learned from Kuecker's example how to admit mistakes and talk about them more openly. Kuecker learned from Wetstein's example how he could work with gays and lesbians notwithstanding the teachings of his own religious background. Each changed in ways he had not imagined, because they allowed themselves to have a relationship based on mutual self-interest and respect. By the end, their power increased, and each grew in ways beyond his initial goals. By the end of the campaign, together they were greater than three.

One final note: It is not enough for us to know that mutual self-interest is the answer; we have to practice it. Think of five people you want to know better—five people you could imagine working with and learning something from. Write their names in the margins of this book. Call them up and ask for coffee. Give yourself no more than forty-five minutes for each meeting. Practice asking tough questions and being direct about who you are and what you want to achieve. See if you can find a spark of mutual self-interest that might turn into an alliance.

In organizing this is called a relational meeting or one-to-one. My mentor told me it takes five years, doing twenty of these meetings each week, before you get good at them. So, no pressure. Take some risks. Make some mistakes. If you can only come up with four names for your list, drop me a line and *I'll* meet with you.

CHAPTER THREE
WHAT DO WE WANT?
AND WHO CAN GET IT "FOR" US?

Give me a lever long enough
and a fulcrum on which to place it,
and I shall move the world.

Archimedes

Action is a public encounter between a group of organized people and someone in power, with the aim of achieving a public goal. Put another way: Action is the moment when we put ourselves to the test. Action is risk.

I learned about action from the Industrial Areas Foundation (IAF). Before linking up with this national alliance of professional organizers, I knew how to protest. I knew how to disobey. And I knew how to help people one on one. I even knew how to advocate for "reform" of the system. But I didn't really know how to take focused, public action that built power and advanced issues.

The IAF teaches that action is to the organization as oxygen is to the body. Without action, the organization suffocates from too many meetings and too much talk. We have all been there —sitting in meetings that go nowhere, talking about why things won't work rather than how to make them work. (Next time you are in one of these meetings that saps your energy, walk out.)

We need real action to survive. And to run an action that's got a shot at achieving something worthwhile, there are four things we need to know: why, who, what you want, and who can get it "for" us.

The first two chapters of this book are about the first two questions: why we fight and who will fight with us. This chapter discusses the next two questions: discovering what we want and knowing who can get it "for" us. (I put "for" in quotation marks, because nobody is going to get anything "for" us that we don't have enough power to force them to.)

The first step in action is learning—specifically, learning what exactly we want (not just what we don't want). Then we move onto learning about our targets—the people who can get us what we want. We put ourselves in their shoes. By the end of this chapter, I hope you will be scribbling in the margins about your next big fight, your targets, and where you might begin.

Chapter 4 will then discuss the only other thing we need in order to act (courage) and the thing to do after you act (evaluate). The rest of the book is about how social change is not quite as easy as this four-step process suggests.

By year two of the Harvard Living Wage Campaign, our team planned rallies like clockwork. Another month, another rally. Who wants to speak? Can we get some professors to come? What time? Who's making posters? We held it at University Hall last time...how about Massachusetts Hall this time?

The problem was we rarely stopped to ask ourselves why we kept planning rallies. If we had asked, we might have come up with the stock-and-trade answers, available to activists everywhere. We might have said we wanted to "increase pressure" or "raise awareness." Or some smartass might have offered, "to get a Living Wage." Not untrue, but not very helpful either. With a few notable exceptions, each of our actions lacked clear goals (what we wanted) and targets (who could get us what we wanted).

There is nothing radical about knowing what you don't want—it is called complaining, and we do it every day. Democracy, rule by the people, depends on us coming up with solutions, not just problems. But too often we let this simple truth get lost somewhere between "I'm pissed" and "Let's do something about it!"

Examples of undirected activity abound. Many outdoor rallies—a common form of protest—lack a well-defined goal. They may be filled with angry people (*who!* and *why!*), but they have only gotten to the point of knowing what they do not want – bad wages, AIDS, job cuts, U.S. in Iraq, a bank bailout, global warming, etc.

So two questions guide our quest for a winnable action. First: what do we want? Second: who can get it "for" us?

Before we begin planning an action, we first have to ask ourselves: "what do we want to achieve with this action?" This question shapes everything else. If we cannot list two or three concrete results we want to achieve from a particular action, then we need to go back to the drawing board. The IAF calls this process "turning a problem into an issue." It involves breaking down a problem that we can't solve anytime soon (poverty, injustice) into little pieces that we have enough power to achieve (25% raise for service workers and a meeting with the presi-

> **If we cannot list two or three concrete results we want to achieve from a particular action, then we need to go back to the drawing board.**

dent of the university), which, if won, would build our organization and leave it stronger to fight another day.

Regardless of what we *want* to accomplish, what we do accomplish relies as much on us as it does on our target—the person who can get us what we want. But it's not simply knowing the name of the crooked legislator or cruel business leader or wicked landlord. The IAF has another saying: "The action is in the reaction." In order to get the reaction we want from our targets, we have to know what matters to them. This requires curiosity, tough questions, accountability. It requires that we humanize them. It's not all that different from the process of mutual self-interest we talked about in Chapter 2. We humanize our targets to understand who they are and to learn how we can work with them. If it comes to it, humanizing them will also teach us how we can press them to do the right thing when they don't want to.

Let's examine these two questions a little longer. What do we want? Who can get it for us?

The first time I really felt anger in public life, it was coupled with shame and disbelief. I was twelve years old and my father was president of my elementary school Parent-Teacher Association. At one meeting, Dad proposed we become a "sister-school" with a school from Dallas—pen-pal programs, field trips, that sort of thing. I had never seen so many people in our school gymnasium. And they were there to protest. Around the time of my dad's proposal, the Texas legislature was pushing through a plan (famously called "Robin Hood") to equalize school funding between rich schools (like ours) and poor schools (like those in Dallas). It seemed fair to me, but I was only a kid. I was amazed when our town reacted with fury and racism. Hate spilled into the debate over my dad's glorified pen-pal program: "You want our kids to give their addresses to kids from the inner-city?"

The sister-school proposal failed. I could not believe it. I wanted to do something about it, but I could not. For years that anger stayed with me, in my stomach. I told the story a hundred times. It was a placeholder for all the time I spent feeling ashamed of where I came from and what little I did to change things.

Thirteen years later, the chance came for me to make amends. In 2005, PACT took up the issue of the inequality of school funding in Illinois. We taught high school and junior high students about the vast disparities (as high as $22,000/year for students in rich districts; as low as $5,000/year in poor districts). Our kids took pictures of leaky ceilings and missing bathroom doors. They collected deflated basketballs and Cold War-era history books. They mobilized local and statewide actions. And they even found ways for suburban kids to help out.

PACT hasn't solved the problem—yet. But the organization has had enough victories on specific issues to remain in the fight. I am confident that if they remain active they will eventually help solve the inequalities in the funding of public education in Illinois.

Issues are packaged in a few basic forms. One is a public commitment from someone in power. If we want more funding for financial aid, our action may be designed to get a public commitment for increased funding from a specific state legislator. If we want better health services on campus, our action may be to seek a public commitment from the head of University Health Services to make two or three specific improvements in problem areas. If we want our apartment building to be cleaner and more attractive to potential buyers, we may seek commitments from our landlord and fellow tenants alike to institute a building clean-up day…in addition to challenging the landlord to live up to specific municipal codes.

These commitments must be specific—clear enough to be worded as a yes or no question: Do you commit to introduce an amendment to the state budget this session for $8 million, yes or no? Commitments must also be public. It is the watchful eyes of 200 voters or three TV crews or a dozen religious leaders that often ensure commitments are made…and, more importantly, kept.

Often we tend to focus energy on the public commitment alone. We must also think about how we are going to make the commitment "stick." Winning the first battle is important, but if we don't also build our organization for the future, there will be nobody left to keep fighting or even to make sure that commitments are kept.

The Voter Power Campaign that united our Muslim, Jewish and Christian bases—along with non-religious groups from City Colleges and high schools—ended up falling short. We threw all our energy into voter turnout as a way to get a meeting with the three primary gubernatorial campaigns. In the end, we got what we wanted—but we did not want enough. We forgot to anticipate what would happen *after* the campaign. We failed to think about how our voting efforts could turn into a long-term foundation for our organization, or how our interactions with the candidates could lead to long-term public relationships. The result: After our big Voter Power Campaign, we spent the next three months re-grouping instead of growing.

Winning the first battle is important, but if we don't also build our organization for the future, there will be nobody left to keep fighting.

Since then, PACT has run a summer internship program for the last four years that has gotten progressively better and more successful. Why? Because the program's goals have become better defined.

Our first year goal was to provide a good experience for someone contemplating a career in organizing.

Our second year goals were to provide a good experience and give the interns a small enough area (a city college, a part of town) to permit them to recruit a base of people who would continue to work after the summer was over.

By the third year, the goal was to develop lasting relationships in very specific young adult communities through voter registration and issue research.

Year four, the internship program sought to build high-level skills and camaraderie among the existing leaders of the organization, each of whom would work on a project or campaign of his or her choosing. Rather than seeking outside interns (who had to learn from scratch and might leave at the end of the summer) we shaped the internship program so it would attract young adults who were already involved in our campaigns. The first year our one intern consumed almost half my time and diverted my attention from other projects. By year four, PACT's sixteen interns served as extensions of its paid staff. They ran actions, won victories around recycling and mentoring programs, and organized new relationships in churches and schools. Rather than siphoning off PACT's resources, our interns multiplied them.

The main thing that changed between years one and four: We knew better what we wanted. As the goals of the internship program became clearer, everything about running the program also became clearer—recruitment, what seminars we would provide, what kind of mentoring was needed, etc.

All good actions or campaigns do two things: win something and make the organization stronger (better able to fight again). The Voter Power Campaign succeeded on the first and fell short on the second. The internship program took four years before it really won anything. Here is a story about wanting more, and getting both.

Antonio Gross is young and black and weighs 250 pounds. He is a college student who still lives in his parents' home. He works at a neighborhood after-school program to make extra money and to encourage kids to follow in his path. He is accustomed to frequent police stops. But in his mind, the police went too far one afternoon. After they stopped him, they made him take his shoes off and lay down on the ground, and they dumped his backpack out onto the concrete. They humiliated him, and then they left, never giving him a reason for their actions or an apology.

Mr. Gross, age 19, got involved in a neighborhood police reform campaign. He liked that our group wanted to bring officers and youth together to start a dialogue, but he was skeptical. He wanted action, not just talk. Action is what he got when we asked him to tell his story of police abuse to the District Commander and ask her to allow youth like him help train her officers.

So Mr. Gross told his story at a meeting of forty or so of his neighbors, and the District Commander listened. Because she could feel Mr. Gross's anger, because she understood the personal truth in what he said, and because she could see the support he had in the room, she agreed 1) to let his group train officers in her district and 2) to make sure officers visited young people in after-school programs like the one Mr. Gross worked for. That way, the officers would get to know young people as people rather than as potential suspects.

This exchange took place at an action in Lawndale, a west side Chicago neighborhood. The original goals of the action were to build momentum for our voter turnout campaign and to use that campaign as leverage for legislative support of our homelessness bill. More voters → legislative commitment. Done. We had no plans of tackling youth-police relations at first. Luckily, we decided to dig a little bit. We wondered if we could get a little bit more out of this action. Maybe we weren't wanting enough. We re-evaluated.

In our original imagining of the action, we had decided that a popular local youth pastor, Phil Jackson, would kick off the event with a rousing call to arms. Neighborhood kids look up to "Pastor Phil." When we re-imagined our goals, we wondered if we could challenge Reverend Jackson to do something different and expand his role as a leader. We talked about how powerful it could be if he told a personal story from his own youth...how a little vulnerability on his part might mean that our other members would relate to him rather than revere him. A personal story like his can help audience members look at those on stage and think, "Hey, I could do that too." Jackson was up to the challenge, and it helped change the tone of the action. Now, in addition to "more voters" and "legislative commitment," we had a third goal: leadership development.

That third goal got us thinking. Which of our other leaders could lead this action as an opportunity to test their abilities? First, that meant adding local homeless youth to the agenda and giving them the opportunity to tell their stories. This demonstration was the right thing to do. It also conveyed what our efforts were really about: Anybody can lead if they are trained and prepared to do so. This new goal of leadership development also led us to Mr. Gross and his issue of police reform. After strategizing with our leadership team, we asked the District Commander to come, almost on a whim, but because we already had a commitment to come from the local State Representative, the District Commander said yes as well. That meant a fourth goal was added: win some real change from the police department.

And once we added police reform to the agenda, it gave us the opportunity to break through some of the tension between west side Blacks and Latinos. Miguel Perez, a 21-year-old Latino leader, had been working on police reform with us for a while. He was not about to miss this opportunity to come face to face with the District Commander who oversaw his neighborhood. His own personal story, and the fact that he was the only Latino at the meeting, reminded our leaders and audience of the need to unify across ethnic and cultural differences.

Incorporating new goals into this action attracted new people to the meeting and helped us unite some of the key leaders from different west side groups. Also, more speakers meant more people got leadership experience for the future. This is how new leaders are born. (One caveat: More speakers at an action only works when those speakers are trained and the agenda remains tight. The meeting above, including a twenty-minute voter registration training, was just fifty-eight minutes.)

By giving many new leaders the chance to speak about their own issues and make their own commitments, we enlisted them as co-conspirators in the voter turnout campaign, which was the original goal of the action. In fact, one of the key legislators who was supposed to attend the action blew us off. But because we were organized and ready, we turned a potential loss into a rallying cry as we gathered signatures for a letter to the legislator on the spot. We were disappointed and we said so. This letter helped us build for the future with that particular legislator (who would regret upsetting a room of young local citizens)—and got our leaders energized.

So all good actions incorporate public commitments and attempts to build for the future. The very best actions also tend to push the organization and its leaders up against their own boundaries and barriers. The hope is that by experimenting we also learn something. Actions can teach us the real interests of an important public figure, whether to test a particular tactic, or provide a bit of information that will help shape a campaign down the road. Sometimes the most important result of an action is what it teaches.

The very best actions also tend to push the organization and its leaders up against their own boundaries and barriers.

For example, in 2006, PACT leaders planned a Leadership Summit. There were two main goals: to get twenty-five new recruits to join a PACT campaign and to build camaraderie and skills across the organization. Susan Lee, age 27, suggested a third goal, "What if we invited some of the public officials we know to come for an hour, just to meet and talk informally with our leaders?"

Normally, we only met with officials to ask for public commitments. But Ms. Lee reasoned that our new leaders might benefit from talking with these officials in a more informal setting, with nothing on the line. The officials might also enjoy the chance to relate to Chicago's next generation of leaders. We did not know whether the idea would work, but we figured it was worth a try. It was a risk, and that's precisely why it was the right thing to do. Organizations need leaders (and organizers) who will push against the status quo and conventional wisdom.

In practice, our experiment was an all-around failure. Of the ten officials who committed to come, only four showed, and two of those arrived late. We were embarrassed. On top of that, one of the officials who did come, Congresswoman Jan Schakowsky, felt that we should have done more to engage her on specific issues.

In all, however, the Summit was still a success. The two main goals were met, and we had tried something new. Leaders enjoyed the opportunity to talk to the officials who showed up, but they realized they needed to take more care confirming attendance and planning some piece of formal business. Lesson learned.

And more than anyone knew at the time, a seed had been planted.

After the Summit, a small team took the initiative to meet with Congresswoman Schakowsky's staff and make amends. These leaders had never worked on a national issue before, but they proposed a follow-up meeting with the congresswoman and a local homelessness coalition on a range of housing issues relevant to the congresswoman's district.

The main goals of this new action were to get the congresswoman to lobby for a housing facility for homeless families and stronger homelessness legislation (public commitments) and to provide an opportunity for two up-and-coming PACT leaders to develop their skills as spokespeople and negotiators. To these two goals, the team added two questions they wanted answered: Did we want to ally more closely with this homeless coalition in the future, and if so, how? And did we want to do the work it would take to build a full campaign around these national issues?

The action was an unqualified success. Congresswoman Schakowsky agreed to both requests, and she was thankful for the work we had done to make our requests so specific—for example, call this member of this committee, and so on. And the leaders answered their questions. A solid foundation was laid for future projects with the anti-homelessness group. And as enticing as it was, they judged they were not quite ready for a national campaign.

Because they built some calculated risk into each of these actions (the Summit and the Schakowsky meetings), our leaders and organizers achieved more than they hoped.

It's not simply: know what we want. It's also: want a lot. And: be willing to risk for what we want.

Jeff Maxwell, 35, wanted to launch a campaign led by ex-offenders like him to create their own new opportunities for jobs and civic engagement. He planned an action outside Cook County prison to launch his campaign and approached a local television station to document the launch. It was such a success that the public access station in Chicago ran it twice a month for a year. This strengthened the campaign by raising its profile in the community. It also attracted more than a dozen ex-offenders who joined the campaign after learning about it on television.

Jaime Jimenez, 19 years old, wanted to get letters signed in support of the Dream Act, federal legislation that would provide opportunities for undocumented young immigrants to attend college. He could have set up a table anywhere and asked for people to write letters—at a train station, his college, etc. But Mr. Jimenez had also been interested for some time in getting youth from his church more involved in the community, so he decided to use the church as the base. His goals for the action were 200 letters of support and five new potential leaders at his church. The letters were written, but only two new people signed up to help. In his assessment of the action, Jaime gave himself a grade of C. He knew that the second goal was just as important as the first.

Let's talk targets. The target of every action is the person who has the power to get what we want "for" us (and it is always an individual person—not "City Hall" or "Starbucks" or "The Man"). Maybe what we want is a new piece of legislation, changing a campus policy, or donating money to support our work. The more we know about the person who can get us what we want, the better.

The primary target of Mr. Maxwell's Ex-Offender Campaign Launch was an alderwoman who had previously refused to work with him and his team because she did not want to be associated with former criminals...even though the goals of our organization were to mentor youth in the community and provide opportunities for ex-offenders to get a job and re-enter society. The alderwoman did not show up for the Campaign Launch as expected, but the action was still a success because Maxwell and others had carved out two other targets: a reporter from the local news station and a cadre of three potential allies (an ex-offender, a businessman, and a service provider) whose support could propel the campaign forward. Maxwell knew these targets well enough to ask them to make their commitments, even without the alderwoman present. The remaining targets all committed themselves to support the campaign. That the action was held in the pouring rain, at dusk, outside Cook County Prison, demonstrated a sincerity that prompted even better news coverage.

The more we know about the person who can get us what we want, the better.

Mr. Jimenez's main targets were the church members, from whom he wanted a public commitment (in the form of a letter to their representatives in Congress) to support the federal Dream

Act. He figured that meeting them after church, face to face, as a fellow parishioner would be enough to get them to act. He succeeded to a degree, but he was frustrated that he had not risked more. What if he had invited Congresswoman Schakowsky to the church or asked his pastor to address the issue in his sermon? What if he had led a march of parishioners to the congresswoman's office and left a ten-foot-tall letter requesting a meeting with her staff? The point is that Jiminez was beginning to ask himself how to best affect the person or persons who have the power to enact the change we are after.

In the meeting with Schakowsky about homelessness, she was the target, plain and simple. Leaders partnered with the homelessness group to research the issue and learn more about her previous record. Because the team knew she had already supported homelessness issues, they focused on how they could push her to commit even more energy to the issue, to move her from supporter to champion. If they had approached her without knowledge of her previous position, they would have appeared ill-informed and disrespectful. Instead, they orchestrated a sophisticated negotiation about what the congresswoman could really accomplish, down to specific phone calls she could make to other U.S. Representatives in Congress.

This meeting also demonstrates why we could-be radicals should move up the food chain as early as possible to seek out the most powerful target. It is not hard to imagine this homelessness team spending months or years planning rallies or fundraisers to raise general awareness for national homeless policies. Instead, they went straight to the person who could get them what they wanted (the congresswoman).

This next story helps illustrate the often-complex interplay between what you want and your chosen targets. It also serves as a reminder that the best way to find out anything (why, who, what you want, or the target) is to try and, sometimes, fail.

Many PACT leaders were angry about the war in Iraq—sad to see their relatives and friends go away, furious about their treatment when they got back. But we did not know what we could or wanted to do about it. There were some in our organization who supported the war outright, hopeful that ousting Saddam Hussein could bring some peace to the Iraqis.

In hopes of clarifying our position, a small group of leaders attended a "Rally Against the War" to learn more about possible routes we could pursue. In order to learn, we took action. Not the other way around. However, instead of learning what we could do, we mostly learned what we did not want to do. The rally had a lot of "why" and "who," 10,000 people yelling (sometimes at each other), but it lacked focus about what we wanted and who could get it for us. It was a mess.

But the rally got us thinking. "What if we had 10,000 people and all these TV cameras? What would we ask for? Instead of railing against what was wrong, what could we actually win?" In other words, what if we had in mind not just "why and who," but also what we wanted and who could get it for us. We posed this question in one-to-one meetings and larger strategy sessions.

The war in Iraq never became a centerpiece of PACT's agenda, but we carved out two related campaigns that accomplished real gains. Reni Soto, 17, was angry that his high school gave out student phone numbers to Army recruiters. Turns out federal law mandates that schools produce this information. But it also mandates that schools provide an "opt-out" for students who want to maintain their privacy. We ran actions on individual principals and found that many did not know their students could opt-out. We met with specific officials within the school district to find out who had the power to change the policy. They were sympathetic. Eventually, at a PACT action attended by seventy-five young people and (unfortunately) little press, Chicago Public Schools' Director of High School Programs announced a citywide opt-out plan. Mr. Soto and others agreed to help publicize the plan.

Another campaign sought better health care for young adults, including military veterans who often lack basic health insurance when they return from combat. Erich Totsch—a young man who had been deployed to the Gulf Region and Kuwait—did not have health coverage and told his story to the Governor of Illinois at an action. A year later, after many smaller actions and continued pressure, the Governor announced that the bill we had written to provide extended young adult coverage would be a part of his plan for increasing health care in Illinois.

Do you remember "Schoolhouse Rock," those twenty-minute educational cartoons? In one segment, an anthropomorphic piece of paper sings a tune about how legislation is made in Washington, DC ("I'm just a Bill, here on Capitol Hill"). Schoolhouse Rock and other programs taught my generation the way the system is *designed* to work.

As an inexperienced organizer, I often fell victim to the Schoolhouse Rock Syndrome. I tended to respond to all problems the same way: Let's write a bill and start lobbying legislators. I was unimaginative and more than a little scared. PACT's leaders eventually taught me that this route is but one of many.

Think back to Jaime Jimenez, the young man who planned the letter-writing action at his church. Though he targeted his Congressional Representative, this was not his only target. He also targeted his parishioners, whom he wanted to engage politically; and he targeted his friends, whose leadership he wanted to build and test.

Or think of Jeff Maxwell, who realized he could do a lot more—build his ex-offender trade school program—without the help of legislators at all.

Or Antonio Gross, who turned a rally for voter registration into a chance to do something about police harassment and profiling.

Or Susan Lee, who came up with a new idea for an annual summit that didn't work out quite the way she hoped but resulted in a new relationship that led to new opportunities.

The best strategy—what do we want? who can get it "for" us?—bubbles up from our "why" and from our relationships with one another. When answering these two questions, beware the Schoolhouse Rock Syndrome, whether it comes in the guise of pressure from outside foundations or so-called experts or our own fears. Or from a singing cartoon.

CHAPTER FOUR
THERE IS ONLY ONE WAY TO LEARN

Ever tried. Ever failed. No matter.
Try Again. Fail again. Fail better.

Samuel Beckett

Watching "The Shawshank Redemption" a hundred times will not make you a great actor. Admiring the toughness of Dwayne Wade will not make you a good basketball player. And reading a book about organizing will not make you a successful organizer. I have tried all three. There is only one way to learn: first by taking a risk and then by evaluating the result.

I was angry when I wrote the following words in my journal: "My first job is to act. My second job is to act. My whole job is to act. I don't build trust and then act; I act so that I may build some trust. I do not raise money and then act; I act in order to identify the donors I really want. I don't endure boring meetings to build credit; I build credit by walking out. I do not learn unless I act. Every week, take a risk. Then, every day. Then, every conversation."

I wrote these words fueled by an anger born of regret. Six months into my job as a community organizer, I was stuck obsessing about the opportunities I had missed simply because I had been too afraid to act.

When William Faulkner was asked what he thought he could teach young writers, he responded: "I don't think anybody can teach anybody anything…. The young writer that is, as I say, demon-driven and wants to learn and has got to write…will learn from almost any source that he finds. He will learn from older people who are not writers, he will learn from writers, but he learns it—you can't teach it. Then I think too that the writer who's actually hot to say something hasn't got time to be taught. He's too busy learning—he knows what he wants—his instinct says to take this from this man or that from that man."

Faulkner's description works equally well for us could-be radicals as it does for could-be writers (Faulkner's gender bias notwithstanding). We must be "demon-driven"—that is, we have to understand our "why." There must be something inside us that compels us to take action, to try and make things happen. Without this inner-strength, we will bounce around from ideology to ideology or from mentor to mentor without developing a center of our own.

We must also nurture relationships with people who are different from us. We do not learn from our prescribed teachers alone. We can learn from "almost any source." We must throw ourselves into the process of learning through real-life experience and action.

My favorite phrase from Faulkner's quote is that the young writer is "too busy learning." It evokes a different idea of learning than we are accustomed to. Real learning flows from action as much as it does from study and contemplation. It flows from "instinct" as much as from intellect. And it is brought about by the learner, not the teacher.

This chapter is about a very specific kind of learning—learning through action plus evaluation. Once we know the why, the who, what we want, and who can get it "for" us, our work as could-be radicals is well underway. The rest is marshaling the courage to act and making the time to evaluate our action. This chapter is first about courage and second about evaluation. We need both.

The rallying cry of the fearful is "we need to wait until we are ready." It can also sound like this:

- "We cannot do a sit-in aimed at our university president; that's too controversial, and we are too weak. We don't know if we have the support of the student body."

- "We cannot meet with state legislators yet; we don't know whether this issue matters to them, or what will make them respond to us."
- "Is this even allowed?"
- "We can't do this. We don't know the consequences."

When we have a tight-knit, passionate group that knows what it wants and who can get it, what the above statements often mean is: "We are afraid." Fear makes us throw up barriers to action.

Fear is a serious thing. The answer to fear is not to simply brush our concerns aside or mask them with machismo. Instead, we can use our fears to make our action better. A good action is not good because it ignores fear; nor is it good because it waits until fear is overcome. A good action is good, in part, because it addresses fear head-on.

Let's break down the four statements above to help understand why and how we might choose courage.

"We cannot do a sit-in aimed at our university president; that's too controversial, and we are too weak."

This first statement was made at a meeting of the Living Wage Campaign in January 2001. After two years of protests, research and outreach, Harvard University had barely budged on our demands for better pay and labor practices for campus employees. On top of that, one of the Harvard trustees had just publicly declared the living wage issue "closed." We knew we had to react in a big way, and we developed three possible plans of action:

- Option 1. Do a protest, linking arms around the site of the next meeting of the Harvard Corporation (essentially the school's Board of Directors). We would demand to make a presentation at the meeting.

- Option 2. Link arms outside the meeting and not let them in, forcing the Corporation members to meet with us outside.
- Option 3. Do a full-fledged sit-in in the President's office to show our commitment, force a meeting, and draw media attention.

Even though Option 2 was the worst option—complicated, unlikely to succeed, coming from a point of weakness—it attracted the most support during our strategy session because it seemed like a compromise: a little more risky than the first but not as risky as the third. Smart people in the organization did not believe we could pull off the sit-in; something of that magnitude seemed beyond our capability. We were afraid.

The deliberations shifted, however, when some of us seniors, seeing our time left on campus dwindling, advocated for the sit-in. Our courage emboldened others, and the vote ended up almost unanimous. For the next two months, the action itself (the detailed planning, the recruitment, the hushed phone conversations) completely energized the campaign. Fifty-two people risked their academic standing and agreed to sit-in for the planned three-day action. An almost equal number planned rallies to create support from outside the building. Even though the sit-in ultimately lasted twenty-one days, we didn't waiver. The IAF says "Action is to the organization as oxygen is to the body." In other words, do not wait until you have support before you act. Act in order to build support.

In hindsight, those people who had argued that we were too weak to do a sit-in were correct when they said it. It was not until we decided to act, to risk, that we had the strength to pull it off... and win. The sit-in was the turning point in negotiations with the university. A year later, in 2002, students and workers won a wage of $11.35/hour plus benefits.

**"We cannot meet with state legislators yet;
we don't know whether this issue matters to them,
or what will make them respond to us."**

The fear about how our target or opponent would react to us, voiced by a member of PACT, is a natural one. It tells us that we must always be well prepared before we engage someone who has more power than we do. If we do not know what matters to our targets, however, or if we are not sure of the best way to approach them, how better to learn than simply to ask?

Rather than let a lack of knowledge about a target stand in our way, PACT built a special set of questions into virtually all of our smaller actions. Every time we met with state legisla-tors or business owners or high school principals about an issue, we would also ask what was at the top of *their* agenda, how they got into *their* job, and why *their* work was important to them. Doing so might give us an insight into how to work with these people better down the road. Instead of wondering what might persuade our targets, we summoned the courage to ask them.

> **Instead of wondering what might persuade our targets, we summoned the courage to ask them.**

Take for example Illinois State Senator Jacqueline Collins, who came to be a real ally to PACT over time. In one of our meetings with her about financial aid for education, Tangilla Henderson noticed that the senator seemed distracted. She boldly asked, "Senator Collins, you seem mostly frustrated with the rest of the legislature. What is getting you excited these days?"

The Senator brightened. She immediately zeroed in on Ms. Henderson and her question. She talked about two legislative efforts she was spearheading: a piece of legislation to divest state funds from Sudan and a bill to regulate the payday-loan industry. By sheer coincidence, those two problems—Sudanese genocide and unfair lending—had recently been identified by our interfaith team as possible focal points for action. But up to that point, our leaders had not figured out how to approach either issue. Once we shared with Collins our interest in both issues, she helped us develop a strategy for each. When we eventually returned to the financial aid issue, the entire tone of the meeting had changed, and we moved forward with her on all of our requests.

"Is this even allowed?"

Every college has a freshman recruitment day on which student organizations of all stripes woo incoming students. Asian-American Association. Ballroom Dance Team. You name it. Harvard was no different. More than 200 student organizations flooded the yard with free t-shirts, mini-Snickers, and e-mail sign-up lists.

Joseph Basel, a new friend of mine—a fellow incoming freshmen—wanted to start a student volunteer organization on campus, but he had not officially registered the student organization for the new school year. While he was going through the proper channels and learning what it would take to become a student organization (faculty advisor, constitution, budget, etc.), he was told the process would take at least a month. But that was no help to Mr. Basel. The swarm of potential freshmen volunteers were buzzing from table to table. Treasured e-mail lists were being filled up and hoarded. Basel saw opportunity vanishing before his eyes. Then he spied an empty table and two chairs. He simply propped up a hand-made sign, put out two sign-up sheets and started recruiting our classmates.

When I saw what Basel was doing, I asked him, "Is this even allowed?" He responded to my question with a question: "What are they going to do about it?"

If you can, ask for permission. And if you don't get it, do it anyway—and prepare to accept the consequences. We could-be radicals often want everyone to agree with us. Not possible. When you try to do something that will create real change, people will get in your way. When they do, think twice before playing by their rules or filling out their paperwork.

"We can't do this. We don't know the consequences."

During a Red Cross telethon after Hurricane Katrina, recording artist Kanye West told the cameras, "George Bush doesn't care about black people." He was sweating; his voice cracked. I assume that what went through his mind before he said those words was, "I can't do this. I don't know the consequences."

Do I agree with Mr. West's famous quote about Bush? Not fully, but I think it contains some truth. Would I have said it myself? Probably not. But his statement might have been the best thing to happen on television that year. My favorite part was the look on West's face. It was the look of someone who knows he is taking a risk. He must have had a million reasons not to say those words. After the Dixie Chicks debacle of a few month's earlier, he must have known the world had little tolerance for musicians with political views. But he said it anyway.

West's action is a good lesson about courage. Actually, perhaps the only redeeming quality of his action was courage. All in all, it appears he did little in the way of research or preparation. Not only was his action poorly planned, my guess is that he failed to evaluate the action afterwards. (The fact that he has since become less involved in social issues, rather than smarter and more involved, makes me fear he did not spend much time thinking about what happened and learning from it.) Nonetheless, his honesty and courage touched a nerve with millions of Americans, myself included. His was the highest-profile racial critique of the handling of Katrina up to that point. In the following weeks, more criticisms and better-coordinated actions emerged. But maybe they all owed something to this one flawed but courageous act.

Courage, the willingness to risk, is every new generation's most valuable resource. We will always be outmatched in money, clout, and institutional strength. But courage we have in spades. As the saying goes, we are too young to know better. Older generations know of our courage all too well. Often with the best intentions, they spend our courage on war or they undermine our courage with cynicism. We do not have to let them. Just ask Dan Kelly and Bailor Barrie.

Two hours after getting off his plane from the U.S. to Sierra Leone, Dan Kelly was committing himself to starting a clinic in a country where the only person he knew was the person with whom he was having the conversation, Sierra Leone native Bailor Barrie. Mr. Barrie, a local young doctor, had the ideas and the local know-how. Mr. Kelly thought he might be able to find the money and resources. They were both too young and foolish to doubt each other's sincerity or accountability.

Little by little, the two young men built the clinic. Before long, hundreds of rural Sierra Leonans were counting on the two of them to make them well. They all (Barrie, Kelly, and the villagers) needed supplies. They needed space. They needed know-how. They needed a corporate structure. They needed government approval. Their risk had created responsibilities. As each new challenge arose, they met it.

Three things separate Kelly from your average white American do-gooding foreigner. One, he built his work on a reciprocal relationship with Barrie. Two, he and Barrie took risks. Three, the two of them stuck around long enough to learn from their mistakes and hold themselves accountable for the responsibilities their risk had born.

Kelly still struggles with his role as an outsider who does not plan to stay, and Barrie struggles with his own aspiration to leave Sierra Leone and study medicine abroad. To their credit, they don't struggle abstractly; they struggle in the thick of trying to treat real patients and create local solutions to real public health problems.

This chapter is not only about action but specifically about how action serves learning. The Harvard Living Wage Campaign took the better part of four years because we kept making the same mistakes over and over. In that campaign, learning and evaluation happened only at the margins; or for me, only years later.

How can action serve learning? How can action and evaluation be part of the same whole? Mike Gecan, a longtime organizer and supervisor with the Industrial Areas Foundation, discusses the good "habits" of a citizen's organization. I like the word *habit* because it implies doing something repeatedly—to the point where it becomes a part of you. Mr. Gecan identifies the habits of *relating* and *acting*. He also identifies the habit of *evaluating*, which might be the most important habit we could-be radicals can learn—specifically because it allows us to keep on learning.

A good evaluation is an honest assessment of how an action or meeting went. It includes a quick survey of those who led the action: "In one word, how do you feel right now?"

The evaluation includes an assessment of goals. "When we planned this assembly, we said we wanted to get a commitment to train police officers, attract ten new leaders to our campaign, and get press coverage from the local paper. How did we do on each of these things?"

The evaluation includes high points and low points. This is where lessons are really learned—by lifting up the example of leaders who did well and offering critiques on things we could have done better.

Finally, the evaluation includes a brief discussion of what happens next. A good evaluation not only makes for smarter individual leaders; it also makes us a stronger, smarter, hopefully more unified group of leaders. We collectively pass judgment on an event, and that judgment leads us to a collective next step.

Evaluations are also the way we honor the precious resources our supporters give us—their time, money and effort. This is why effective could-be radicals take meetings seriously. Meetings are only called when there is an action to be ratified. Our meetings last from forty-five minutes to an hour. They start and end on time. Meetings have agendas that are worked out a week or more in advance and that take into consideration the multiple interests of those present. When we put this much effort into our meetings, we owe it to ourselves to take an extra fifteen minutes afterward to evaluate how it went. (If we do not put this much effort into a meeting, we should cancel the evaluation anyway. There is no need to evaluate a disastrous, unorganized meeting.)

One of my organizing colleagues was running the evaluation

for a meeting that had been co-chaired by Andy Chen, a relatively new leader in PACT. The meeting itself was designed for people like Mr. Chen who wanted to learn how to start organizing in their own communities. Chen himself had been dragging his feet some in terms of his own commitment. But, in the heat of the meeting, he went with his gut and decided to share his frustration with the rest of the group. He touched a nerve; his honesty clearly helped others in the group understand that their struggles were not unique.

The evaluation is the time to build upon not only what went well but what could have been better.

Watching all of this transpire, my colleague made sure to spend a good part of the evaluation focusing on Chen. She asked him how it had felt to be at the front of the room, and she gave him credit for taking the risk to share his frustrations. The evaluation gave Chen a chance to take some credit for leading and also to see that other people were now looking to him for guidance. As important as Chen's comments in the meeting had been to others, it was the evaluation that solidified his confidence and resolve.

As we have discussed, a good action involves the courage to take risks. In other words, built into every good action is the possibility that it will go badly. The evaluation is the time to build upon not only what went well but what could have been better.

Deonna Adams, a 20-year-old nurse-in-training, had helped bring ninety-two young people from PACT to a public meeting between then U.S. Senate candidate Barack Obama and United Power for Action and Justice, an IAF-related organization in Chicago. Her delegation of ninety-two people formed part of an audience of roughly 1500 people. Though the action achieved its goals—the audience got commitments on important issues, and the young adult delegation made a small but important contribution to the agenda—Ms. Adams felt uneasy afterwards.

At the evaluation, she said, "I want to be able to do that," referring to the entire 1500-person action, "by ourselves." Others in the group started nodding in agreement. They all wanted the power not to simply piggyback on the work of others. They wanted their own organization. The evaluator used this frustration as the framework for discussing what the group might pursue next: "What would it take for us to get there?"

Courage, the willingness to risk, is every new generation's most valuable resource.

Two months later, the energy harnessed in that evaluation led to a commitment to plan a campaign of 100 house meetings—small group brainstorming sessions in schools, coffeeshops, and religious institutions across Chicago—to build an agenda based on issues affecting young adults and attract the leaders who could make real change happen. This effort would become the foundation for successful campaigns on health care, financial aid, and police reform.

We evaluate after actions and meetings. We also evaluate in the course of our face-to-face meetings with potential leaders and allies. Often, more emerges in these settings than in a more formal evaluation.

On the evening of Election Day 2006—the culmination of PACT's campaign that mobilized 13,774 young voters—those who led the campaign were exhausted. They half-watched election returns at a local pub and passed around plates of nachos. They talked about anything but voting. The evaluation was brief and uninspired. Everyone said nice things about each other and spoke vaguely of the pride they felt. Nothing more.

Over the next four weeks, however, leading up to PACT's monthly leadership meeting, a few themes emerged from one-to-one conversations. Folks were tired. Many felt like they were on their own in their neighborhoods; they wanted help. They did not want to lose the voting campaign's momentum. These feelings culminated in a proposal to spend three months digging in our neighborhoods to find the next generation of leaders. We would use the success of the Voter Power Campaign as a credential. This internal, re-energizing campaign helped people take stock; it provided a jolt of new energy for the organization. Their honest assessments in face-to-face meetings had protected them from burning out.

One final point on action and evaluation. We must each find a mentor—someone who cares first and foremost about our development. It can be a boss or employer, but—be careful—a mentor must be more worried about *us* than the work we are doing for or with them. Be careful to avoid the temptation to have lots of mentors. We need many advisors and allies and comrades, but our mentors are the ones who commit to a regular meeting, at least once each month. They are the ones to whom we routinely write a report organizing our thoughts. We could-be radicals take mentoring seriously (either as the mentor or mentored), because there is no better opportunity to impact another individual outside our own families.

A successful campaign for some sort of recycling program

in our neighborhood, for example, may affect 3000 people in a small way. But the people we mentor will call us five years from now asking our advice on the decisions that continue to shape their lives.

Evaluation is the basic nature of a mentoring relationship. A mentor asks us how we are doing and why. A mentor challenges us to be the person we want to be. A mentor reveals our flaws and our skills. A mentor makes us ask what comes next.

Richard Bach wrote "we teach that which we most need to learn." The only thing as helpful as finding a mentor is finding someone to mentor. My favorite moments in organizing took place when I was trying to teach someone else the same things I was trying to learn myself.

My mentor, Ed Chambers, gave me a hard time for the better part of a year about being too much "in my head," about my using big words or ideas when stories would be more effective. He would say, "Tell me from here [pointing to his heart] instead of from here [pointing to his head]." I found his advice charming and clever the first time I heard it, but I came to loathe his refrain. Until I became a mentor myself.

When Joy Friedman came to meet with me, I had nothing to lose. She was only going to be in town for two months, and she wanted an internship with PACT. I asked her why she wanted to work with us. She started rattling off her resume and talking about how important she thought it was to fight poverty locally and abroad. She was speaking from her head. "Tell me from here [I pointed to my heart] instead of here [my head]," I said, hardly believing what I was doing.

Ms. Friedman paused for what seemed like a minute. I felt like apologizing, but before I did she responded with a description of the personal struggle that helped fuel her anger about the way women are treated on her campus, in her adopted city, and in other countries she has visited. She started telling stories. The meeting changed in that moment, she got the internship, and the lesson about head and heart finally stuck with me.

A radical is someone who unites with others in the world-as-it-is to bring about the world-as-it-could-be. Action is the step radicals take to move from one world into the other. Like Rene Delgado pressuring a state senator for extra commitments. Like Scimone Edwards mustering the temerity to speak in public for the first time. Like Jeff Maxwell returning to prison in order to vow never to go back.

We actually have a hundred little opportunities to act every day. Asking someone a question we are afraid to ask. Sticking up for a friend when it's easier to stay silent. Confronting someone who's done us wrong. Even choosing to preserve family time when work is piling up. These actions are rarely as dramatic or successful as the examples above, but their defining characteristics are the same: They are all difficult, and the result of each is uncertain. As we seek to change the world and ourselves, we need to beware of easy fixes and try to develop an appetite for what's difficult. We must keep returning to that uncomfortable space in-between the two worlds. We have to make our mistakes…and then learn from them.

This chapter in brief: Take action, then learn from it. The book so far:

- Start with what makes you angry.
- Find someone to help you fight.
- Decide what you want (your goals), not just what you

don't want.

- Plan an action aimed at the person who can get you what you want.
- Summon the courage to go through with the action, no matter what.
- Evaluate at every step, preferably with a mentor.

We are almost ready to go make some mistakes. Before we do, however, let's start in our own backyards. When our anger derives from a very *personal* experience (being evicted by a landlord, failed by a local principal, faced with a family member's medical struggle), our anger sustains longer. It puts us in a better position to communicate our passion to others and ask them to be vulnerable with us about their passion as well. We want a world where all people stick up for themselves; let's start by sticking up for ourselves. This way, we will be better equipped to say what will make the situation better, because we are judging for ourselves (rather than for someone else). We will be more likely to know the people who can get us what we want, because the problem is more likely to occur within our own communities. And because our aim is ours, the courage will be more readily accessible.

CHAPTER FIVE
IT TAKES A WHOLE BODY TO ACT

In public life,
the senses are what allow us to act.
Otherwise, we get so tied up in thinking,
that the opportunity to actually
do something passes us by.

Edward T. Chambers

Sometimes we could-be radicals mistake intellect for action. We explain simple things with big words and esoteric references to make ourselves seem smarter than we really are. We use knowledge or intellect or awareness to exclude. We choose friends and colleagues who agree with us. We are more concerned with what someone thinks than what someone does.

The fact is that we learn just as much with our bodies as with our brains. It takes a whole body to act, or as Ed Chambers says, "The body trumps the brain."

Citizen organizations often run what are called *house meetings* (five to ten people at someone's home) to learn the interests of a community and attract new leaders. PACT did 127 of these meetings to build its original issue agenda. At the first one, to get the conversation going, our host asked: "What is an injustice you have experienced in your own life that you would want to fight against?"

Anita Andrews-Hutchinson, a black, 29-year-old entrepreneur who oversaw a daycare center among other businesses, answered first. She went into depth about her experience of growing up as a student in Chicago public schools, often without necessary supplies. She talked with passion about wanting something different for her own baby.

Before she finished, however, one of the traditional activists in the room interrupted her to say, "Well, you can't talk about public education without talking about the military-industrial complex." Within a couple minutes, this young man and his hyper-intellectual "analysis" had sucked the energy out of the meeting. The new people were intimidated, Ms. Andrews-Hutchinson was insulted, and no one else felt like sharing a personal story afterward.

So, what is wrong with being too much in our heads? What is the alternative?

Some of the best things in life—eating, sex, naps, birth, dancing, music, laughter, love—have little to do with our intellect. Intellectuals do not dance better or laugh harder or love their families more than others. At best, our minds help us evaluate and communicate how to get better at these things. At worst, our minds can distract us from appreciating the best stuff. The truth is somewhere in between. Our task is not to deny our minds; rather, it is to use our minds in concert with the rest of the body.

Our task is not to deny our minds; rather, it is to use our minds in concert with the rest of the body.

Our education tends to separate and elevate the workings of the mind (intelligence, information, discipline) over the rest of the body (physicality, passion, anger). Meanwhile, Facebook, Twitter, MySpace too often take the place in our lives of the intimacy of sitting across from another live person. It's strangely hard to get all of us—heart, body, mind, gut—in one place at one time.

Let's talk about heart. Curiosity and vulnerability come from the heart. It is my heart that makes me feel like crap when you feel like crap, gives me joy when you feel joy, feeds me energy when you are energized. One of the responsibilities our generation has as could-be radicals is to make the business of politics more human.

Our face-to-face relational meetings are a particularly fertile ground for practicing heart. Try this: Schedule a one-to-one relational meeting with someone this weekend. For this one meeting, focus not on the words that are spoken but on your partner's tone of voice. Approach the meeting as you normally would, just focus more on his or her voice. When does the voice rise or fall? Mumble? Garble words? Speed up? Slow down? Change pitch? What does this tell you about the person?

In your next meeting, be most mindful of the expressions on his or her face. The time after that, concentrate on body language. Practice using your whole self when you are in conversation with someone. And, by the way, turn off your cell phone!

Joel Zuniga, a 19-year-old technology wiz who aspired to join the Marines, knew about heart. Alongside other young leaders in PACT, he had scheduled a meeting with representatives from the mayor's office on a series of issues (education funding, youth homelessness, and the city budget). The meeting looked like it would be a showdown: four young adult leaders and four staff people from the mayor's office staring at one another across a boardroom table. On the mayor's turf, no less.

The meeting had only been agreed to by the mayor's office after a larger group of 325 young adults had tried to sleep inside his office to get his (and the media's) attention about a range of proposals to reduce youth homelessness. Our group had real business to get done, but we were worried the mayor's representatives would be more concerned about our previous tactics.

Mr. Zuniga had another idea. He suggested that we start the meeting with a very short introduction and then split off so that we could have four individual face-to-face meetings—our education leader with the mayor's education rep, our budget leader with their budget official, and so on. We would become four pairs instead of two factions. The rest of us agreed to Zuniga's plan. It worked. Paired face-to-face, the mayor's staff started to see us as we were: thoughtful young people who cared deeply and wanted to get things done. PACT got what we wanted and began to build stronger relationships with the mayor's office.

In the evaluation, each of our leaders talked about the tension they felt early in the meeting and the change that occurred when our counterparts got to meet us as "four human beings." For that to happen, we had to use our entire bodies—all our senses, instincts, intuition—to pull off the action. We refused to argue about tactics or even issues. We went for a relationship between two human beings (times four), and it worked. It was heart in action.

Heart's one thing. Gut's another. Gut is where courage and disgust (and anger and hunger and sex and laughter) come from. It is also where violence comes from. Rather than try to cultivate this powerful, passionate body part, our culture usually tries to suppress it. In action, gut often gives us the courage to speak up when even when our mind want us to shut up.

Gut is easy to practice on your own. After your next encounter with someone, think of a question you wish you would have asked but were afraid. Meet with that person again and ask the question you were afraid to ask the first time.

Another way to practice gut is to learn how to pay attention to your stomach. Here's one thing my stomach taught me: Stop lying.

Relationships are built on trust. Trust only happens when people take action together over time. Trust is hard to build, but is easy to lose. Trying to make myself look better, trying to get results fast and easy, I would lie when the truth was less convenient.

My regrettable favorites:

- The Rose-Colored Lie: "We normally have twenty-five people at our planning meetings." The Truth: The most we ever had was twenty-five.

- The Exaggeration: "We passed legislation to regulate pay-day loan stores." The Truth: We held one lobby day and got a couple more co-sponsors onto a bill that would have passed without us.

- The Near-Truth: "Yes, Senator, some of our leaders have been working on that issue for some time." The Truth: Me and one other person in the organizations are interested.

- The Self-Aggrandizing Lie: "I speak a little bit of Spanish." The Truth: The last time I strung together two Spanish sentences was 1998.

- The Lie of Encouragement: "Great job! I'd give your action an A-minus." The Truth: Turnout was low, the meeting ran thirty minutes late, and you did not get a real commitment from your target.

- The Lie of Convenience: "Public transportation is a mess today. I will be there as soon as I can." The Truth: I lost track of time, as usual.

- The Lie of Cowardice: "I won't be able to make it to your house meeting tonight. I am not feeling well." The Truth: I'm scared about working in a new neighborhood with new people of a different race. Why would they listen to me?

After every lie, my stomach felt rotten. But that didn't stop me from getting away with my lies. Most people trusted me, and those who were skeptical were probably liars like me anyway. Case in point: Every six months or so I would hear about "the next big thing" in youth organizing. The story rarely varied: hundreds of young people...youth-led...winning major campaigns...with little or no money...etc. Unfortunately, the story was always not quite true. People just believed so much in what they were doing that they got carried away. Just like I did.

I've been told by some colleagues that lying is part of organizing. Done in moderation, the theory goes, lying keeps the troops happy and saves face with the powers that be. When you are trying to win victories alongside young (or poor or working) people, isn't it worth it? For my part, as my confidence as an organizer grew, my lying stopped. So did the rot in my stomach.

Gut is much harder to practice collectively. Here is the story of two young adult leaders who were only able to go off-script because they had rehearsed extensively. Their team had talked through various situations and built up enough mutual respect to take a risk—and go with their guts—with the knowledge that they would be supported.

Access to health care unified a diverse group of young people in Chicago—religious leaders, artists, former veterans. Fifty percent of all young people in the United States are without health insurance at least once between their nineteenth and twenty-nineth birthdays. Having written legislation to expand coverage to more young people, PACT faced opposition from the health insurance lobby. These companies would actually have benefited from the legislation, but not as much as they would benefit from another plan that would have hurt young people (by reducing the number of guaranteed medical benefits). It took some time, but PACT leaders got a meeting with the CEO of one of the insurance agencies. They wanted these two things: good statistics from the insurance industry about what their bill would really do and a commitment that the company would not oppose our bill.

Even though they prepped for two weeks, our leaders could not anticipate all that would happen. To open the meeting, the insurance company representatives, smiles wide, presented each of the young leaders with a complimentary pen, complete with the company's logo. It was patronizing. (One thing we could-be radicals need to learn is that we are always fighting two battles: one to win the issue at-hand and another to simply win respect.)

Chava Goldstein, 26, wanted to make sure that the representatives knew she and her cohorts meant business. She listened to her gut. After the representatives finished shaking hands and distributing pens, she quipped, "All we brought were agendas." Everyone laughed (albeit for different reasons), and the momentum for the meeting swung back in our leaders' favor. Later on in that same meeting, 28-year-old Brandon Havlick's gut started telling him that the meeting was too technical. He asked for permission to interrupt. He took two minutes to tell stories of friends who worked in the artistic community and could not get insurance through their jobs. Mr. Havlick's words also helped shape the tone of the meeting.

The action succeeded because two of the leaders followed their instincts. The company agreed to provide the research and withdraw opposition to our bill, at least for the moment. The CEO mentioned that he had children who would be in a similar position if he were not the head of a big company.

Physicality can be the difference between keeping and losing control of a meeting. If we do not have the time or money to take acting or dancing lessons, there are other ways we can learn physicality in public life. Where and how can we practice using our entire bodies to act? Almost anywhere (except on the phone or the Internet).

Rene Delgado is the student I described earlier who decided to work on financial aid instead of health care or immigration because his best friend could not afford to take care of her children and go to school at the same time. Eventually, Mr. Delgado was selected by his peers to speak at an action to confront an Illinois state senator and ask for support on financial aid. Delgado was to make his speech and then make three public demands of the senator. She had committed to only one of these three requests in a pre-meeting, so Delgado knew he had to give a first-rate presentation. The problem was that he simply could not stand still when he spoke in front of other people. In his nervousness, he would stutter and shuffle and shift. So he practiced and practiced and practiced.

On the night of the action, Delgado put two pieces of tape down on the floor behind his podium to remind him to keep his feet still. He got up and told his story to the assembled 210 young adults. He took his time and conveyed the seriousness of his message by standing perfectly strong and still. After he finished, he paused. Then he turned his entire body to the senator and said, "Madam State Senator, we have some questions for you. Please stand." He was no longer a young activist meeting with a public official for the first time. He was a serious political actor with an audience of 210 potential voters in lockstep behind him. The senator committed on all three items.

Another reason Mr. Delgado's speech worked so well was because of the venue. He and other leaders thought they would have about 175 people, so they booked a room with a capacity of about 125. When 210 showed up, the energy was palpable.

People in power understand the importance of physicality and drama. They put judges on high benches, city council members around a dais, politicians on platforms and podiums, governors and presidents and bishops in mansions. Corporations build massive skyscrapers and jockey to place their products and advertisements at eye level in stores. What the establishment can buy with money, we could-be radicals can make up for with numbers. It was harder for the senator to say "no" to 210 organized young people in a small church than it was for her to say "no" to five of them in her own office…or even to 210 of them in a hall that holds a thousand.

Sometimes, doing absolutely nothing with your body is an action in itself.

Physicality is something to use in collective action, but it is also something to keep in mind for encounters as cozy as our one-to-one meetings. The next time you are in a coffee shop, watch people as they talk to each other. You will see patterns. For the most part, conversations contain a combination of nodding and smiling. Both parties are normally engaged with each other, leaning forward. Rarely do folks openly disagree or even withhold approval of one another. By changing your posture or by withholding your approval until someone says something that truly moves you, you can shake up the normal dynamic.

About six months into my job, I noticed that I would share more of my insecurities than I intended with my mentor, Ed Chambers. Even though I would start our meetings with an agenda of bullet points, I inevitably found myself delving into my worries and frustrations. Why?

The answer was stillness. If Chambers didn't like my questions, he wouldn't answer. Whenever he thought I might be holding something back, he would just sit and wait. Eventually, I would fill the silence with whatever was on my mind. He taught me an important lesson. Sometimes, doing absolutely nothing with your body is an action in itself.

Organizing taught me that if we want to use our whole body to fight for what we believe in, we have to take care of it. Eat well. Sleep. Exercise. Read. Turn off our cell phones when we get home. Take time for ourselves, whatever that means for each of us. (If you do not know what it means to take time for yourself, find out.) In short, we could-be radicals must rest from the work. Instead, we too often do the opposite. We brag about who among us is most busy, most committed, most "hard core." We argue over who got the least sleep and who has the most on his or her plate. We joke about drinking too much coffee and forgetting to eat lunch.

Do not fall for this "self-destruction arms race." We gain no insight into making the world better for other people by treating ourselves like crap. Ben Wikler, 28, has worked in almost every high-stress profession from talk radio to global advocacy to a senatorial campaign. He says that when he is frustrated at work he first looks at three things: what he's eating, how he's sleeping, and whether he's exercising. Usually one of these is the culprit. If so, he fixes it. If he's eating, sleeping and exercising just fine, he knows it must be the job itself. And he then fixes that.

One PACT leader, Jessica DeVries, 23, goes outside to blow bubbles when she is stressed out. She also relies on her roommate and other close friends to remind her to spend time taking care of herself so she does not get bogged down by her work.

When I asked Ms. DeVries to develop a new ten-minute

training for other members of a community organizing class on anything she wanted, she decided to focus on the challenge of getting enough rest. After she gave her classmates the opportunity right then and there to blow bubbles with her (to her surprise, most went along and even enjoyed it), DeVries asked all of them to write down one or two ways they take care of themselves. She then told them to pick one and actually schedule it into the next week. Finally, each classmate took responsibility for reminding one other classmate to do the same thing. Even rest is something for which we can hold each other accountable.

Earlier we discussed how 1 + 1 can be greater than 2. When you and I combine, not only can we accomplish more together. We may also challenge each other—as Matt Wetstein and Ahmed Zedan and Max Kuecker did—to change and become more than what we each started with.

The problem with this formula is that it assumes that we all bring our whole selves to our endeavors. Most of the time, we are less than one. We are distracted. We are tired. We are using our words, but not our hearts and stomachs. The same can be said for our actions. We fail to imagine with our whole bodies what a campaign or a meeting or a project could be.

Take Ms. DeVries' lead. Scribble down a few things you would do for yourself if you had the time. If one of the things you wrote was "reading," turn this page. If not, come back later.

CHAPTER SIX
MAKING HISTORY

Helped are those who create anything at all,
for they shall relive the thrill
of their own conception
and realize a partnership
in the creation of the Universe
that keeps them responsible and cheerful.

Alice Walker

Faulkner was asked how he develops his characters in his novels. He said he finally gained that skill "after about ten books." Becoming an effective agent of change does not happen overnight. This chapter is about how achieving change takes time, power and judgment.

Chapter 1 argued that it takes years to learn our "why," and then it keeps changing. Chapter 2 extolled the virtue of relationships, which by definition only get built through action over time. Chapter 3 reminded us to keep making mistakes until we figure out how to zero in on what we want and who can get it "for" us. Chapter 4 offered stories about the only tool that can come quickly (courage), but reminded us that courage is only valuable with constant evaluation. Chapter 5 focused inward on our hearts and guts, our whole bodies.

This chapter focuses our attention outward. Here we ask, "How does history get made?"

In Spanish, the word for power, *poder*, means "to be able." As a verb, it is something that you do in the moment, rather than something you have. To act with power is a skill that becomes a craft that becomes a means for collective expression on the scale of art. We call this art form "politics."

Politics is a web of negotiations among different interests. Power, if achieved by a collective and used with wisdom and imagination, is the source of the greatest advances in the history of civilization. When power is instead given away or wielded violently, it is also the source of humanity's greatest failures.

To teach other could-be radicals about power, I sometimes run an activity that goes as follows: I hold up a plain white sheet of paper with the word *power* written on it. I ask everyone in the room, one by one, what they would do if they had the power to make a change in their neighborhood. I listen to each answer, and afterwards, I reply, "That sounds like a good idea. But I have the power."

Frustrated, eventually a few members of the class will get out of their chairs, corner me, and grab the paper. There are two main lessons to be learned from this activity:

1. Power will not be given to us. We must take it.
2. It's very hard to get power by yourself (i.e. the more people involved, the easier it is to wrest the piece of paper from me).

But participants often learn other lessons as well. One group spent nearly ten minutes talking about how someone really ought to take the sheet of paper away from me before anyone actually had the courage to go ahead and do it. In their evaluation, they added these two lessons to the ones above:

3. You cannot get power from talking.
4. No one will get power for you.

In another instance, the participants became particularly angry with me for lording my supposed power over them. They added this lesson:

5. Those who do nothing with their power are jerks.

Most of us know that we need power (to change things), but we are also afraid to have it (because we have seen it do such bad things). Our temptation is therefore to avoid power and its trappings, but we can choose to master it instead.

How do we master the art of politics? Where to begin? Like most art forms, politics is largely misunderstood. We consider it the purview of experts, pundits, politicians, lobbyists, charismatic leaders. That is, it is someone else's job. Just as we have professional musicians, baseball players, and comedians, we have professional politicians. In this kind of climate, the opportunities for inexperienced young people like you and me to wield power can seem few and far between.

As a result, most of us, most of the time, become "political spectators," resorting to watching politics—rather than exercising power. We watch CNN. We read the morning newspaper and gossip about politicians' successes and failures. We talk about politicians similar to the way we discuss celebrities. We want to know what's going on in the world but are not sure we want to be part of the "game." We think we know what is right or wrong in our heads, but we don't often do something about it. We like the comfort of knowing all about "national" issues (war, health care, stimulus packages)—but their distance from our daily lives makes it easier for us to justify our inaction. At our worst, we become spectators who use our superior knowledge to make other people feel uninformed. At our best, our spectatorship just means we are on the way to action but not sure where to start.

By contrast, the "political hobbyist" takes action, but only on special occasions. Political hobbyists are political spectators who take some action, but not on a regular basis. Like the avid vinyl-record collector or the guy who does graphic design on the side, we dabble. We vote. We support a friend or colleague who is running for office. We occasionally write letters or distribute petitions. We read and respond to e-mails from MoveOn.org or Focus on the Family or Barack Obama's permanent campaign. We occasionally encourage our churches or businesses to do the right thing. We political hobbyists think of ourselves as "voters" and "volunteers."

When we sit down to share our stories with other political

hobbyists, they will say things like "give me a call if you need any help with anything" or "what you are doing sounds great, but I don't know if I have the time." When we are in the mindset of a political hobbyist, we react. We have a healthy skepticism about politics but prefer to spend our time earning a living and hanging out with our friends or families. When we do take action, we form the hands and feet of major political movements. We are the everyday people whose individual actions add up to something greater.

Finally, some of us will choose to practice politics as "political craftspeople." We craftspeople make the choice to develop our skills over time. We are like the hobbyists, but we add in time and discipline. We are the leaders and professional organizers who make up grassroots political organizations. Craftspeople develop and run campaigns that sometimes take years to win. Within those campaigns, we maneuver and re-organize. We know the tools of recruitment and training and institutional development and direct action; we have learned how to use these tools through practice and subsequent evaluation. We avoid making repeated mistakes in favor of making new mistakes.

Like the dancer who attends lessons from childhood or the doctor who devotes seven years to study, we politcal craftspeople are serious about learning the skills needed to succeed.

Like the dancer who attends lessons from childhood or the doctor who devotes seven years to study, we are serious about learning the skills needed to succeed.

We could-be radicals must give ourselves at least five to ten years to learn the craft of politics. These are not five to ten years of waiting to act. It means acting now, achieving what we can now, and learning along the way. It means learning from doing. Learning the craft does not simply mean "being involved" in social justice. It means taking action and evaluating that action, over and over. In the words of Samuel Beckett, describing another craft, "Ever tried. Ever failed. No matter. Try Again. Fail again. Fail better."

Learning the craft of politics means finding a regular mentor who challenges us and reads our reports. It means finding other models and heroes in public life and learning from them. It means choosing our enemies as carefully as we choose our allies. Learning the craft means doing one-to-one relational meetings over several years with people who can show us something different and asking: "What can I learn from this person?" and "What can I teach this person?"

Learning the craft of politics means developing the habit of evaluation. It means evaluating with others after every meeting and every action and finding time on our own to evaluate ourselves. It means recognizing the smallest things: the personality trait of a friend, the kindness of a bus driver, the way one neighborhood looks compared to another.

Learning the craft means reading everything from *The People's History of the United States* to the *Tao Teh Ching* to *The Invisible Man*. It means reading Hannah Arendt and Saul Alinsky and Ayn Rand and Alice Walker and Kurt Vonnegut and Dave Eggers. It means finding authors who seem to be writing your innermost thoughts, as well as other authors who seem to be writing in a foreign language, because their ideas are so different from yours.

We must become the author of our own thoughts. We must write letters and journals and blogs and books—not because we have to but because doing so forces us to ask and answer basic questions about who we are and what we are struggling to accomplish.

And we could-be radicals must lead. Leaders have the ability to move and motivate others. We could-be radicals do not need charisma, though most good leaders do have confidence. They know what they want. They relate to others. They act. They evaluate. They use their whole bodies—head, heart, gut, physicality. They know how to use power collectively with wisdom and judiciousness. They know how difficult it is to exist in-between the world-as-it-is and the world-as-it-could-be, and still they return to that basic tension.

One potential leader, Nate Garrity, age 23, got involved with PACT in large part because he wanted to unite three churches in his neighborhood. Early on, Mr. Garrity tried meeting with leaders of these institutions in hopes of bringing them together to support various justice issues. He even tried brokering a relationship with another outside organization to help develop a coalition. He failed—they brushed him off. Garrity lost this fight but found other things that he cared about and could actually win. He spent the next two years honing his craft and built up a group of other young followers from his own church.

Two years after his initial effort, the same three churches decided on their own to start organizing together around local social justice issues. Because Garrity had demonstrated his leadership and built up a following, this time they called him to ask for his help. Meanwhile, the outside organization he originally contacted was also recruiting him...and a national foundation had called to see how it could support his work.

Garrity had devoted himself to learning his craft. Over time (the only way it could have happened), he became one of the respected leaders in his community. Not only did this give him the opportunity to make the changes he originally sought, but he was able to do it on his own terms. Stick around long enough and you become the longest-standing leader: This is one of the many lessons that can only be learned over time.

▼▼▼

Occasionally, political craftspeople attain brief moments of transcendence. In these moments, the accomplishment is so profoundly personal, yet so transformational, that it deserves a word greater than craft. We become "political artists."

There is no formula for achieving politics as art, but it usually contains elements of the emotional, the dramatic, and the transformative. Politics often becomes a numbers game that gets lost in budgets and proposals, votes and dollars. Political artists can change the game by adding emotion.

If politics is the art form of the radical, transformation is the goal. Transformation from anger to action, transformation from interested to engaged, transformation from the world-as-it-is to the world-as-it-could-be. To achieve transformation, radicals rely on their imagination.

The mayor of Chicago is Richard M. Daley. Daley, a six-term office holder, is the son of Richard J. Daley, himself a six-termer immortalized in books such as *Boss*, *Clout*, and *American Pharaoh*. Every summer, the current Mayor Daley holds three public hearings about the city's annual budget. Anyone can attend and get a brief audience with the mayor. One by one, citizens go to a microphone and give criticism or testimony. As they speak, the mayor sits about twenty yards away, surrounded by his key staff members. And he says nothing. People ask the mayor all kinds of questions (some rhetorical), but Mayor Daley has mastered the art of silence. He simply waits for each person to sit down. Sure enough, after a while they do just that.

Twenty-two-year-old Ayinde Jean-Baptiste of PACT supported an investigation into the Chicago city budget to study how much money went to young people and whether the budget was environmentally and fiscally sustainable over time. He came to one of these budget hearings to ask the mayor for his cooperation with the investigation (by making his top budget official available to our group) and to agree to meet with us at the culmination of our investigation.

Mr. Jean-Baptiste knew that most of the speakers would be older, representing only themselves, long-winded, sometimes disrespectful, and unlikely to wait for an answer from the mayor. He decided to do the opposite. He approached the microphone, stated his name, and briefly credentialed himself by listing the communities that he and his organization represented. He said a word about the work young people were doing to support the investigation and why. Then he said: "Mr. Mayor, I have two questions. I will wait for an answer to both. First, will you agree to make your top budget official available to us for our research, yes or no?"

Then he waited. The mayor waited. Mr. Jean-Baptiste waited some more. It took some time, but finally the mayor fumbled with the question until Mr. Jean-Baptiste repeated it. Eventually, the mayor gave an exasperated "yes." The budget official himself even stepped in to help answer the question by volunteering his services to the group.

This little action by Jean-Baptiste and his team worked because it transformed the nature of the hearing. He had crafted the evening's first moment of silence, and it got the mayor's attention.

This action also shows that we could-be radicals must learn how to operate in the world-as-it-is, not just the world-as-it-could-be. In the world-as-it-could-be, the mayor would have taken everyone's questions. But, of course, he did not. He responded to Mr. Jean-Baptiste's political artistry.

Occasionally, political craftspeople attain brief moments of transcendence.

When Jean-Baptiste and his colleagues left the hearing to evaluate, however, they spent little time appreciating their victory. Mostly, they were angry at the way the Mayor had avoided making a commitment to some of their requests. And they were unsure about whether his one tepid commitment would lead to much. When politics reaches the level of art, it often has the discombobulating effect of offering a transformational moment but also reminding us how much is left to do.

Being judgmental is bad. That's what I thought. Organizing changed my mind.

Turns out judgment, like power, is good if we make good use of it. The question is not whether we judge, but how we judge. By judgment I mean deciding what something is worth. Since we could-be radicals are in the business of uniting human beings for action; judgment often means deciding what *people* are worth. It sounds cruel, and if done carelessly, it is. To be sure, judgments can be bad. My own missteps are instructive here.

I have used judgment as a defense mechanism: "That group

may be good at raising money, but it's only because they compromise their principles more than we do." I used it to manipulate: "Such-and-such person needs a job, and I can convince him that being involved in our group will help him get one." And I used it to badmouth: "You better stay away from that guy; he's a manipulator who is only interested in promoting himself."

I also passed judgment on myself. I spent much of my second and third years in Chicago convincing myself I was not cracked up to be a professional organizer. I made the judgment that my failures and flaws were insurmountable. I wasn't diligent enough. I wasn't detailed enough. I was too much in my head. I was a coward. These judgments kept me from learning and growing better and faster; they also kept me from enjoying my job as much as I could have.

The question is not whether we judge, but how we judge.

So how can judgment be good? It is good in the formula followed by Catholic Action in previous generations: "Observe. Judge. Act." Observe what is really going on. Judge what needs to be done. Act to make things better. Latin American liberation theologians embraced this formulation and used it to encourage peasants to stand against unjust colonial rule. The formula can also help us could-be radicals understand the importance of judgment in our work.

As the Catholic Action formulation suggests, judgment is no good without observing and acting. Observing means allowing ourselves to be affected by the world and the people around us as they really are. Observing is a generous thing, a close relative of empathy.

Action is our attempt to move one step closer to the world as it should be. Action is a decisive thing and, as we have seen, it takes our entire bodies to accomplish successfully.

Judgment happens in-between the observation and action. Judging helps us sort through the possibilities and potentialities. It helps us prepare for action. And judgment surely goes awry when it loses either of its cohorts. Without action, it is aloof. Without observation, it is vicious.

Even if our judgments are accompanied by observing and acting, however, they still can be wrong. I learned this the hard way.

To find PACT's first crop of young leaders, I conducted more than 2500 face-to-face meetings in neighborhoods across Chicago. If I judged that someone was capable and interested in building a new organization for young adults, I kept pursuing him or her—offering the person opportunities to attend trainings, develop campaigns, and mobilize locally. While I rarely excluded anyone outright, I certainly pursued some people more than others.

Fast forward two years. We had had minor success with financial aid and health care campaigns, and we boasted a solid core team of twenty-five strong leaders. Together the leaders and I decided we were ready to hold a founding convention to officially launch our new organization. We wanted to eventually turn out 1000 people for the convention, so we planned a summer action to build momentum. Sort of a warm-up.

For the summer action, we strategically chose a location downtown, right outside the governor's Chicago office. We had a tight agenda that would highlight commitments from public school officials and legislators. We prepped seventeen young adult speakers who would tell their stories and outline their plans of action. At the end, we would triumphantly announce our founding convention and invite the governor to attend. Our turnout goal for the warm-up action: 250.

Exactly fifty-three people showed up. We went ahead with the action (probably a mistake), but what had gone wrong?

Our problem was my bad judgment. In pursuing that core group of leaders, I had made the mistake of looking for people who were like me: book-smart, middle-class, optimistic young people who did not have much of a following. (Many of the leaders, like me, were not Chicago natives.) We all had rather sunny dispositions, but not enough grounding in our neighborhoods and institutions. So not only were we bad at turnout, we were also reluctant to call each other out about it.

After this fiasco, it was clearly time to try something new. At the next meeting, two of our leaders led a session teaching the rest of us how to identify new people and institutions who could attract even more people. They offered a little tough love, but mediated it by breaking us up into pairs so everyone had a partner to rely on.

For my part, I started going back to some of the folks I had written off earlier. I worked up the courage to approach more established groups, whom I had assumed would not be interested in joining something so new.

As a result of this last-minute tweaking, the PACT Founding Convention was something of a mess. Working-class blacks and white Evangelical college students turned out in big numbers, but these communities were not yet integrated fully into our leadership. As one observer put it, "The people on stage didn't match the people in the pews."

We anticipated this, and in an attempt to help remedy the situation we broke with our established tradition to let two new leaders speak from the podium, even though they had not attended the mandatory rehearsals. Both went over their allotted time and veered from our agreed-upon platform. So we failed doubly.

But we did start and end the meeting on time. And 1083 people (out of 2000 estimated beforehand by our overly optimistic leadership) showed up despite the snow. We got significant commitments (and a measure of respect) from the governor of Illinois, the CEO of the Chicago Public Schools, and a handful of other legislators and officials, all of whom attended. The *Tribune* and the *Sun-Times* both covered us.

Roughly seventy-five young people planned and executed that Founding Convention of PACT in Rockefeller Chapel in 2006. But 1083 attended, bused from all over the city to help usher in this new organization. Those 1083 were young adults who had been mobilized to action. They believed in one of the issues we were taking up or they wanted to be a part of a group taking on the governor and the CEO of the Chicago Public Schools. The 1083 gave PACT the power to convince the governor and the press to attend. They gave energy and excitement to the seventy-five leaders that day and continued to support these efforts in churches and on campuses afterwards.

Eventually, some of the 1083 became the next seventy-five PACT leaders. Did we make history? We'll let you know in twenty years.

AFTERWORD
WHO WILL DECIDE
OUR GENERATION'S LEGACY?

**The future belongs
to those who prepare for it today.**

Malcolm X

Who will decide our generation's legacy?

The wage and wealth gaps are widening. As more of us lose our jobs and end up below the poverty line, we spend less time voting and engaging in issues. As questions are increasingly decided by an elite few, we do the math and figure our influence is insignificant. Even so-called "progressives" seem happy enough now that their guy is in power instead of the other guy.

This book is written for young, could-be radicals, people who want to make a life's work of changing the world—starting in our own backyards. But in a world of almost seven billion people, does it even make sense to build power democratically at a grassroots level, one person at a time?

When many of us see the variety of paths in front of us, we choose those that will let us skip past the whole democratic part of social change. We drift toward "national" and "international" advocacy organizations and policy shops that have no local base. We become social entrepreneurs in the spirit of the dot-com entrepreneur—seeking the silver bullet idea that will fix the whole system. We want to make millions in finance (or win the lottery) in order to eventually give some or most of it away. We confuse blogging with action.

But these are not our only options.

The spread of grassroots organizations in the U.S. and other (relatively) free societies represents a massive, burgeoning movement that is largely overlooked. More notable than the election of a man who spent a mere three years as a community organizer is the slate of meat-and-potatoes victories racked up by commuity organizers in the last thirty years. Just within the Industrial Areas Foundation network of broad-based organizations in some fifty cities and towns, democratic grassroots power has achieved the first ever living wage ordinance in Baltimore, orchestrated universal health care in Massachusetts, built 4,000 affordable homes in New York, and challenged the entrenched political cultures in California, Texas, Illinois and other states.

Increasingly, national solutions are borrowed from successful local experiments. And no one is experimenting with as much success as these dynamic local citizen organizations. What's more, community organizations are also taking the responsibility of training everyday citizens to keep growing their power. Their timeline is not every four years; it's generation by generation.

The powers-that-be still respond to an organized group of everyday people, no matter what their age.

Most of the young leaders who helmed PACT in Chicago came to grassroots organizing with skepticism. We wanted to make a significant difference, but we assumed the challenges presented by our age and lack of resources would stand in our way. We assumed that the height of our success would be to provide a training ground for young people who might be able to appreciate these lessons later in life, not in the here and now.

Instead, we came to learn that the powers-that-be still respond to an organized group of everyday people, no matter what their age. This is partly because of how rarely these powers encounter groups like ours. Our ammunition—personal stories, votes, moral high ground, smart direct action—still goes a long way.

At best, those in power, like the rest of us, are moved by the stories of people who face adversity and seek redress. At worst, people in power, like everyone else, are moved by the threat of losing their jobs or having their inaction outed on the front page of a newspaper or website. Like the movements and leaders whose shoulders we stand on, we could-be radicals were able to achieve real change in the public realm too.

Who will decide our generation's legacy?

Isolated policy wonks and pundits and bloggers? A new generation of philanthropists who buy influence with money? Barack Obama?

Or will it be you?

ACKNOWLEDGMENTS

In the four years I spent building PACT in Chicago, I learned a trade I love (organizing). I studied under a legend (Ed Chambers). I met and married a woman who makes me a better man (my Sara). And I helped start something that just might last.

But I left. I left Chicago and organizing. I left to spend more time with my wife and for the chance to live overseas. I also left because organizers are supposed to leave; we hand over the organizations we build to people who can take them in new directions. *So the organization continues to be led by its local leaders—not by any single person.* This is what I was taught at that very first IAF training, and I got used to repeating it in the months leading up to my departure.

But I also left because I wanted to get out from under the job long enough to see it for what it was, to see myself for who I am. I wanted to evaluate.

This book is what I found. Grassroots organizing of the kind we tried to practice in Chicago really does have some magic in it. It is, as Saul Alinsky said, "the fire under the boiler of democracy." It is simple yet difficult, but anybody can do it. It is not so much about information or money as it is about time and courage. When it's good, it's personal as hell.

The lessons of organizing stick with me: trust your instincts; listen; be honest. Organizing has taught me I could do *anything* and talk to *anybody.* And it taught me to rely on other people, which is why this book has been through more than a dozen readers and revisions.

I owe Ed Chambers for the opportunity to prove myself in Chicago. I owe him for my newfound gut and honesty. This book is dedicated to him.

My parents Mark and Jane Smith, two of my favorite writers, read the book over and over and claimed to like it more each time. Neither of my parents is religious. They put their faith in people and in the possibility that things can be better. They put a lot of that faith in me.

Allison Ondocsin, my little sister, is an inspiration to me. She was the first person to teach me what it means, and what it takes, to fight for something. I look up to her.

To all of the leaders whose stories are told in these pages, thank you. On rare occasions, your names and neighborhoods are obscured to protect your privacy. But your courage unmistakably shines through. Khalilah Worley, Mike Rodriguez, and Matt Wetstein deserve special credit for making the book smoother, smarter and truer.

Tim King, the book and I owe you much. Thank you for your commitment to it and for your hunger to read new drafts. And thank you for helping lead PACT after I left.

Most of the victories PACT has won came down to the leadership of a small group of people. You can read this two ways. First, take joy in the fact that a small group is capable of great things. Two, appreciate just how hard it is to combine in larger numbers. I was hired to build PACT from nothing into a powerful, unified alliance. I didn't get there. When I left, we were still a collection, not a collective. Thank goodness I put the fate of PACT in the hands of Amy Totsch. Amy, you are world-class. As far as I can tell, you are making lots of mistakes. Keep it up. And thank you for pressing me to include in these pages more about judgment and about the frustrations of could-be radicals.

Josh Blanchfield, you are the best kind of friend. With your help, as you have done many times, you have reminded me who I am and what I might aspire to become.

Tom Lenz, you inspired me to let my guard down. You reminded me how tough this work is and how any good book about change must capture all the doubt inherent in doing something unknown.

Greg Pierce, my editor and publisher at ACTA Publications, thank you for your patience and commitment. You taught me how to write a book. Thank you for taking a risk and helping make this dream come true. Without you and your staff, including designers Tom Wright and Patricia Lynch, this book is still sitting on my home computer and not in this reader's hands.

Sara Natania Whitaker, you are my true love. Thank you. Without you, I would just be me.

More Praise for **Stoking the Fire of Democracy**

Through a compilation of honest dialogue, storytelling, and experiential anecdotes, Stephen Smith provides a practical handbook in relationship building, risk-taking, and organizing for social change. A terrific read for anybody who dares to question the status quo, refuses to accept the world-as-it-is, and seeks to create a world-as-it-should be.

> *Andrew Rabens, Presidential Management Fellow,*
> *U.S. State Department*

As an Evangelical Christian, my faith in the liberating essence of collective action and the importance of human dignity has been furthered by *Stoking the Fire of Democracy*. Stephen Smith provides a prophetic vision of the power of actualized human potential and shows that everyone has something to offer. This book not only gives me hope in the world as it could be, but provides a glimpse of what it actually looks like.

> *Josh Dickson, National Recruitment Director,*
> *Teach for America*

Stephen Smith's personal anecdotes and methodical outline to grassroots organizing offer any young organizer insightful perspectives on the risks, rewards and lessons of a life dedicated to social change. *Stoking the Fire of Democracy* goes to the heart of the power of mutual self-interest in empowering both the organizer and his or her community. Smith employs his firsthand experiences to illustrate a universally transferable strategy based on the questions we must ask to find what drives us all toward collective action.

> *Felice Gorordo, Co-Founder and Chairman,*
> *Roots of Hope, Inc.*

Stoking the Fire of Democracy is a must-read for anyone who aspires to be a catalyst of change. Stephen Smith writes in the same way that he encourages others to lead—with an obvious passion for his cause and an appreciation for the importance of details. He focuses on big ideas while littering his book with relevant examples from his and others' experiences in order to teach not only from their successes but also from their failures. This book is not just a how-to manual for the aspiring radical. It is the bible for any young person who wants to change the world. It also presents the author and reader with a unique opportunity for personal reflection. Smith describes his own experiences with a level of vulnerability and honesty that is disarming. He encourages others to lead by example and he has done exactly that.

Michael Housman, Wharton School of Business

Stephen Smith analyses the how, why, when, and with whom that must be worked out in effective community activism. He has written a sharp, readable manual for beginning activists. It's straight from the hearts and minds of campaigners for the Obama Presidency and the early years of the "Yes, We Can" man himself. If you want to leave things as they are, do not buy this book.

Peter Loizos, Emeritus Professor,
London School of Economics and Political Science

Stephen Smith grounds philosophy in personal experience and guides passionate youthful intentions into action. Before reading ***Stoking the Fire of Democracy***, I struggled to know how I could turn my passion into a grassroots campaign. He introduces a brilliant framework that minimizes pitfalls and allows for reflection. Whether we embark, engage, or evaluate, this book serves all— could-be radicals and radicals alike.

Dan Kelly, MD, Founder,
Global Action Foundation

The genius of American democracy, in de Tocqueville's words, is that it enables "freedom as the principal means of action." How will the post-Obama generation choose to act? Stephen Smith's *Stoking the Fire of Democracy* is a deeply introspective book that is highly applicable to anyone in our generation searching for the tools to remake America.

Dr. Federico Baradello, Co-Founder, Thirty Summit

Stephen Smith takes us on a personal journey in his quest to seek out his rightful role within the movement for unity, peace, justice and equality for all. This book is a must-read for young activists who are searching for answers for how to put theory into action.

Rudy Lozano, Jr., Educator and Community Activist

Other Resources on Organizing

BEING TRIGGERS ACTION
by Edward T. Chambers
The executive director of the Industrial Areas Foundation mulls about the nature of being and action, and wonders what it is that keeps people from acting effectively in public life. 40 pages, paperback, $5.95

THE POWER OF RELATIONAL ORGANIZING
by Edward T. Chambers
Ed Chambers mulls about the building of relationships in public life that allow us to share our values, passions and interests with one another as a prelude to action. 33 pages, paperback, $5.95

THE BODY TRUMPS THE BRAIN
by Edward T. Chambers
Chambers mulls about how humans learn with all their senses, including instinct and intuition, and how our education system tries to downplay what he calls "social knowledge" in favor of academic exercises. 48 pages, paperback, $5.95

EFFECTIVE ORGANIZING
FOR CONGREGATIONAL RENEWAL
by Michael Gecan
The author of *Going Public* and one of the directors of the Metro Industrial Areas Foundation describes how the tools of organizing can and are transforming Protestant, Catholic, Jewish and Muslim congregations. 54 pages, paperback, $5.95

ROOTS FOR RADICALS
Organizing for Power, Action and Justice
by Edward T. Chambers
Chambers' "big" book on organizing demonstrates how IAF organizations are making connections across differences of nationality, culture and class. 152 pages, hardcover, $18.95

**Available from booksellers
or call 800-397-2282 for information on bulk discounts.
www.actapublications.com**